THE AMERICAN EXPERIENCE
EXPLORING
AFRICAN AMERICAN HISTORY

by Kathryn Wheeler

CARSON-DELLOSA PUBLISHING COMPANY, INC.
Greensboro, North Carolina

CREDITS

Editor: Carrie Fox

Layout Design: Lori Jackson

Inside Illustrations: Bill Neville, Lori Jackson

Cover Design: Peggy Jackson

Cover Illustration: Rob Mayworth

TABLE OF CONTENTS

EXPLORING AFRICAN AMERICAN HISTORY

A TIME LINE OF

AFRICAN AMERICAN HISTORY

1619–1777

1619
A Dutch ship carries 20 Africans to Jamestown, Virginia.

1640
The trial of John Punch takes place.

1662
Virginia passes the "condition of the mother" slavery law.

1770
Crispus Attucks, a black sailor, is killed in the Boston Massacre.

1773
Phillis Wheatley's *Poems on Various Subjects* is the first book of literature by an African American to be published.

1777
Vermont is the first U.S. territory to abolish slavery.

1793–1847

1793
Congress passes the first Fugitive Slave Act.

1800
The first "official" Underground Railroad routes are established. (Date is approximate.)

1808
Congress makes it illegal to "import" slaves from Africa.

1820
The Missouri Compromise is passed.

1829
David Walker publishes his *Appeal*, a book urging a worldwide rebellion of slaves.

1847
Frederick Douglass starts publishing the *North Star.*

1850–1863

1850
The second Fugitive Slave Act is passed, along with other compromises, to balance slave and free states.

1852
Uncle Tom's Cabin by Harriet Beecher Stowe is published.

1857
The Supreme Court issues the Dred Scott decision.

1861
The Civil War begins.

1862
Robert Smalls steals the *Planter* and gives it to the Union Navy.

1863
The Emancipation Proclamation takes effect on January 1.

A TIME LINE OF

AFRICAN AMERICAN HISTORY

1865–1881

1865
The Civil War ends. President Lincoln is assassinated.

1865
Reconstruction begins.

1868
The 14th Amendment is ratified, granting citizenship to African Americans.

1870
The 15th Amendment is ratified, giving African American men the right to vote.

1875
The Civil Rights Act of 1875 is passed.

1881
Tennessee passes the first jim crow laws.

1883–1957

1883
The Supreme Court overturns the Civil Rights Act of 1875.

1896
The Supreme Court decides *Plessy v. Ferguson*, which establishes the "separate but equal" standard.

1954
The Supreme Court hears *Brown v. Board of Education of Topeka* and rules school segregation unconstitutional.

1955
Rosa Parks is arrested for not giving her bus seat to a white man.

1957
President Eisenhower sends federal troops to Little Rock, Arkansas, to integrate Central High School.

1963–2003

1963
Martin Luther King, Jr., is jailed and writes his "Letter from Birmingham Jail."

1964
Poll taxes are abolished by the 24th Amendment. The Civil Rights Act of 1964, outlawing segregation of public accommodations, is signed by President Johnson.

1965
Literacy tests for voters are abolished by the Voting Rights Act.

1968
Martin Luther King, Jr., is assassinated.

2003
The Supreme Court upholds affirmative action in a case involving the University of Michigan.

Slavery in America was an evolving system, not an unchanged institution that was the same in the 1600s as it was by the eve of the Civil War. Many shifts took place in the system during slavery's existence in colonial America and then in the United States. This unit will help explain these changes to students.

First, it is important to understand the difference between indentured servitude and slavery. An indentured servant had an agreement with his or her master for a specified period of time. During the indenture, the master virtually "owned" the servant. The servant did all of the work that the master required. At the end of an indenture, the servant was freed, usually with some goods or land to start a new life. In Virginia, a typical indenture termination included a grant of 25 acres of land, a small house, grain for planting, and a cow. With these things, the servant could start a new life as a free person.

Slavery, on the other hand, never ended. A slave could not look forward to freedom, a house, or a tract of land. A slave was a servant for life, always living under the orders of a master.

In the early colonies of America, such as Jamestown and New Amsterdam, there was a mix of indentured servitude and slavery. Many Africans were actually indentured servants, not slaves.

In fact, some scholars think that in Jamestown, there were no actual slaves when the colony was founded; instead, slavery evolved as landowners started to understand the value of servants who never had to be freed.

In New Amsterdam, by contrast, the first slaves in the colony had a very different life from slaves who lived in America 100 years later. These slaves used the Dutch court system to ask for wages for extra work; to demand plots of land for farming; and to obtain other rights, even though they were slaves. Eventually, the Dutch colony instituted a system called "half slavery" in which slaves could become independent farmers, even though they were still bound to work for masters when called upon. These slaves had freedoms that their grandchildren could only dream of.

During the 17th century, conditions for slaves started to change. In Massachusetts in 1641 and in Virginia in 1661, lawmakers began to pass laws to legalize and define slavery. One Virginia law stated that if a child was born to an enslaved mother, that child also became a slave with no hope of eventual freedom. This was a major turning point. Although some slaves still managed to obtain small freedoms for themselves, overall the system of slavery was solidly in place by 1700.

For part of the 17th century, slaves were able to use the court system to gain some freedoms for themselves and their families. Then, stricter laws concerning slavery eroded those freedoms. This activity is designed to help students understand what it means to have freedoms and what it might feel like if they were taken away.

FOLLOW THESE STEPS:

1. Before beginning this activity, discuss each freedom listed on page 11 with students. Tell them that some of the freedoms are important in their own lives today. Others may not apply to their lives now but probably would have been very important to them if they were slaves.

2. Distribute copies of the reproducible on page 11. Ask each student to choose the five freedoms he wants most and rank them in order of importance starting with number 1. Ask each student to write a short sentence explaining why each freedom is important to him.

3. Remind students that slaves in New Amsterdam were able to use the Dutch court system to gain some freedoms for themselves. Be sure that students understand that all of these freedoms, which are basic rights for Americans today, were special privileges for slaves. Explain the difference between a right and a privilege. Then, tell students that the courts have granted them only the freedoms they ranked 1 through 3. Ask them to look at their lists and discuss the following questions:

☞ Does the fact that they cannot have all of the freedoms on their lists change their minds about what they think is most important? Do they wish they had ranked their freedoms differently?

☞ What would it be like to live without the other two freedoms on their lists? Be sure to have students talk about what makes each freedom important. For example, many slaves wanted to work for money so that they could buy their freedom.

☞ How do they feel about getting the first three freedoms on their lists? Have students imagine what their lives as slaves would have been like without these freedoms. How will these new freedoms change their lives for the better?

4. Consider allowing a day to elapse before moving to this step. Announce to the class that the laws about slavery have changed. The courts have decided to take away freedoms 2 and 3 from slaves. Now, each student is only granted his most important freedom. Ask students to look at their lists and discuss the following questions:

☞ How will their lives change now that their second and third most important freedoms have been taken away? For example, if one freedom they lost is the right to grow food, how will this change how they eat? Will they be hungry? If they were selling food for money, how will losing this freedom hurt them?

☞ In what ways is it harder to have a freedom and have it taken away than never to have had the freedom in the first place?

5. The next day, tell students that all of their freedoms have been taken away by the courts. How do they feel? What will their lives be like now?

6. Ask students to write individual responses to the activity. Or, write a story as a class about a slave who is forced to live without any of the freedoms on the list.

In the early days of the American colonies, black people faced different situations in various geographic areas. But, most of them were able to negotiate some freedoms, and many of them were indentured servants, looking forward to being freed one day. In 1640, an event in Virginia started a change in laws that eventually deprived Africans of their rights. Hugh Gwyn, the owner of a small plantation, had three unhappy indentured servants. They plotted together and ran away. When they were caught and brought to court for punishment, the African, a man named John Punch, was punished much more severely than the other two men, who were white. Explore this court case with students.

FOLLOW THESE STEPS:

1. Make copies of the reproducibles on pages 12 and 13. Give each student a copy of the Venn diagram on page 12. Tell students to complete the diagram as you read them a story.

2. Read the following text to students:

    In 1640, a man named Hugh Gwyn had a small plantation. He had three indentured servants. All three were men. All three were farm workers. One was named James. James was from Scotland. One was named Victor. Victor was from Holland. The third servant was named John Punch. John was from Africa. James and Victor were white. John was black. All three men did the same work on Hugh Gwyn's farm. They all worked in the fields. They all slept in the same room.

Hugh Gwyn was not a good master. The three indentured servants did not like working for him. All three of them decided to leave. They knew that leaving was against the law, but they were all unhappy. They made a plan. Then, one morning, they all ran away together. They ran away to Maryland.

The three men were caught a few days after they ran away. All three were taken to court. The court decided to punish the three indentured servants by making them serve longer terms. This meant that each of them would have to work on Hugh Gwyn's farm longer than their indenture papers said.

James had to serve for four more years. Victor had to serve for four more years, too. But, John Punch was told that he would have to serve Hugh Gwyn and then Mr. Gwyn's children for the rest of his life. His indenture would never be over. He would never be free.

3. Have a discussion period after the reading so that students have time to finish their Venn diagrams. After students have completed their diagrams, give each student a copy of the Student Activity Questions on page 13. Have them use their Venn diagrams for reference.

4. Discuss students' answers to the questions on page 13 about the case of John Punch.

SERVANTS AND SLAVES

STUDENT READING PASSAGE

DIRECTIONS: Read the story. Then, answer the questions.

When the colonies in America were first settled, not all Africans were slaves. Many of them were **indentured servants**. This meant that a person agreed to work for a master for a set period of time. The master sometimes paid for the servant to come on a ship to America. The servant would live in the master's house. He or she received food and clothing. The master told the servant what to do. Servants could not do whatever they wanted to do. They did not earn wages, or money. A servant could not quit or leave. But after the period of time was over, the servant was freed. Freed servants each received land and a house. They could start new lives.

Being a slave was different. A slave could never be free. A slave was a servant for life.

In America, there were both slaves and indentured servants. Many Africans were indentured.

But, even slaves had some rights at the beginning. In New Amsterdam, which became New York City, slaves used the courts to ask for money for their work. They asked for land so that they could grow food. They were even given something called "half-freedom." This let them live in their own houses. They went to work for their masters when they were needed.

But, freedoms like these did not last. New laws were put into place. These laws made it harder for Africans to be freed. One law said that if a child was born to a slave mother, then that child was a slave, too. One court case turned a black indentured servant into a slave because he had run away. By 1700, slave laws were strict. It was very hard for a slave to have even small freedoms. They lived lives that belonged to other people.

UNIT 1: EARLY SLAVERY IN THE COLONIES
SERVANTS AND SLAVES
STUDENT READING QUESTIONS

DIRECTIONS: Circle the correct answers.

1. Why would someone become an **indentured servant**?

    a. to travel to America
    b. to get land and a house after he was set free
    c. to have work and a place to stay even if he did not have money
    d. all of the above

2. In New Amsterdam, slaves got some freedoms by—

    a. running away.
    b. going to court.
    c. rising up against their masters.
    d. going back to Africa.

DIRECTIONS: Write a short answer.

3. What happened to an indentured servant after the set period of time was up?

    _____

    _____

DIRECTIONS: Write T for true and F for false.

4. _____ All Africans in the American colonies were slaves.

5. _____ Some slaves in New Amsterdam were made "half-free."

6. _____ By 1600, slaves did not have many freedoms anymore.

7. _____ One new law said that a child had to be a slave if his or her father was a slave.

DIRECTIONS: Answer the questions in complete sentences.

8. If you wanted to go to America and did not have any money, would you have become an indentured servant? Why or why not?

    _____

    _____

    _____

UNIT 1: EARLY SLAVERY IN THE COLONIES
WHICH FREEDOMS DO YOU WANT MOST?
STUDENT ACTIVITY

DIRECTIONS: Read the chart carefully. Choose the freedoms you want most. You can only pick five. Then, rank each freedom with your most important freedom as 1 and your least important freedom as 5. Finally, explain why each freedom is important to you.

FREEDOM	RANK (1–5)	WHY IS THIS IMPORTANT TO ME?
having my own room		
seeing my family every day		
getting paid for the work I do		
being able to grow food for myself		
being able to sell food that I grow or something that I make for money		
being allowed to get married		
being allowed to leave the house where I work when I am done working		
being allowed to buy freedom for myself or someone in my family		

Name: _____ Date: _____

DIRECTIONS: Read the chart carefully. Choose the freedoms you want most. You can only pick five. Then, rank each freedom with your most important freedom as 1 and your least important freedom as 5. Finally, explain why each freedom is important to you.

FREEDOM	RANK (1-5)	WHY IS THIS IMPORTANT TO ME?
having my own room		
seeing my family every day		
getting paid for the work I do		
being able to grow food for myself		
being able to sell food that I grow or something that I make for money		
being allowed to get married		
being allowed to leave the house where I work when I am done working		
being allowed to buy freedom for myself or someone in my family		

Name: _____ Date: _____

FROM SERVANT TO SLAVE

STUDENT ACTIVITY

DIRECTIONS:

1. Listen to the story. Fill in the Venn diagram with information from the story.

2. Listen for the answers to these questions:

   • Where did each man come from?
   • Was each man a free man, an indentured servant, or a slave?
   • What work did each man do on the farm?
   • Who decided to run away?
   • What punishment did each man receive?

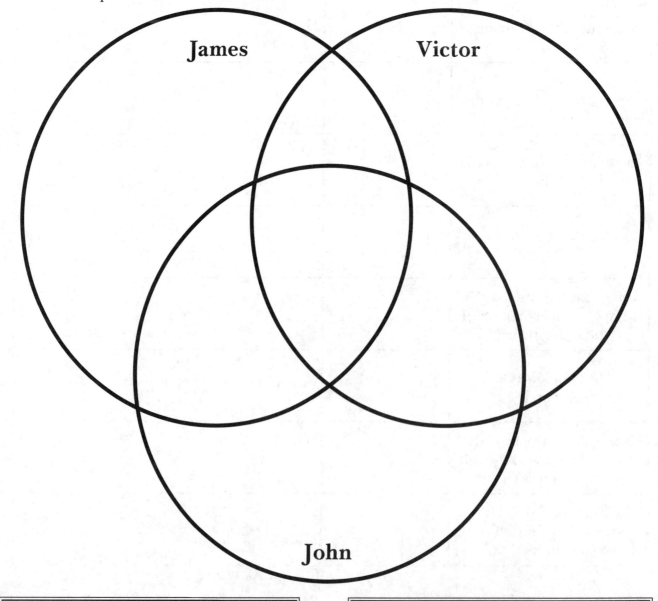

James

Victor

John

Name: _____ Date: _____

DIRECTIONS: Circle the correct answers.

1. Who was John Punch?

    a. a worker on Hugh Gwyn's farm
    b. an indentured servant
    c. a man who came to Virginia from Africa
    d. all of the above

2. Why did Hugh Gwyn take John, James, and Victor to court?

    a. They broke the law by running away.
    b. They broke the law by being unhappy.
    c. They went to England.
    d. none of the above

DIRECTIONS: Write a short answer to each question.

3. When the court ruled that John Punch had to work for life, was he still a servant or did he become a slave? Explain your answer.

    _____

    _____

4. How do you think John Punch felt on that day in court?

    _____

    _____

5. Why do you think the court gave John Punch a different punishment from the other two men?

    _____

    _____

6. Do you think John Punch's punishment was fair? Why or why not?

    _____

    _____

    _____

Slavery continued to evolve in the American colonies after America won its independence from England. Slaves lived in cities, in towns, and on farms. But, slaves were most commonly found on plantations. There are records of slaves working on large farms in the North and in the border states. While some Northern states started abolishing slavery, slave populations grew in the South.

Surprisingly, between two-thirds and three-fourths of all Southerners did not own any slaves. But, plantations had concentrated groups of slave populations. Across the South, there were large plantations with 100 to 250 slaves. Half of all plantations had smaller slave populations of 20 to 50 slaves.

The hierarchy of plantation management usually started with the owner, then moved to a white manager or overseer, and then used black supervisors to monitor work in the fields and on other farm or household projects.

There was also a hierarchy within the slave community. House slaves, who worked as servants in the plantation house, generally had better quarters, were often better fed, and had less exhausting work schedules than field hands. But, few

slaves had a comfortable or easy life. Slave quarters were usually tiny, overcrowded shacks with no sanitation, and slaves were often malnourished. Harsh punishments were used to keep slaves "in line" and keep them from running away.

Sometimes, house slaves were expected to continue working after the owner's family went to bed. Some house slaves' rooms had supplies of extra candles and spinning wheels so that they could spin yarn and thread late into the night. Field hands worked exhausting schedules, especially during planting and harvesting times. All of these things took their toll. Only about half of all slave babies lived past the age of one year. In the 19th century, only about 10 percent of black people in slavery lived past the age of 50.

Perhaps even worse than these conditions was the reality of slavery itself: an owner had complete power over the lives of slave families. At any moment, a slave family could be torn apart when a spouse or child was sold. Sometimes, slave couples lived on different plantations and were given visitation rights. But more often, a sale meant that members of a family would never see each other again. The bravery of slave families in facing this reality on a daily basis cannot be overemphasized.

The owner of a plantation, or master, controlled every aspect of the lives of his slaves. This activity is designed to help students understand what it might have been like to have someone else make decisions about the most basic things in their lives and what it might have felt like to have no influence over those decisions.

FOLLOW THESE STEPS:

1. Distribute copies of the reproducible on page 19. Ask students to read the selections to themselves or have selected students read the entries aloud. (Consider reading the journal selections aloud to younger students rather than using the entries as a handout.)

2. Remind students that slaves were not allowed to make their own decisions about their families, their work, or where they lived. A master's choices were final. Have students discuss what it would be like to have someone outside of their families make all of their choices for them: whether they could go to school, what jobs their parents would have, and what would happen to them and their siblings.

3. Divide students into groups. Assign one entry from the diary to each group. Students will be talking in their small groups about Hector and Betty, Phoebe, Jupiter, or Jesse (and/or the slaves as a group at Christmas). Ask each group to discuss the following questions:

☞ How did a master's decisions affect his slave or slaves? Did he make these slaves' lives better or worse? What would it have been like to suddenly find out about one of these changes?

☞ Imagine, for example, that you are Betty. How will you feel when you can only see your husband once a year? How will Hector feel?

☞ What other choices could a master have made in the case of his daughter asking for a maid? Could he, for example, have chosen a different slave to be his daughter's maid? What might have happened to Phoebe?

☞ Do you think the way that the master plans on treating Jupiter after he catches him is fair? Why or why not?

☞ What do you think of the holiday gifts the master plans on giving his slaves? If you were a slave, what else do you think you would want or need as a gift? Is it fair that the master's manservant, Jesse, will receive a better gift?

4. Have each group present their answers to the class as a whole.

5. Have each student choose one of the slaves to focus on after the discussion is over. Have each student write a first-person story about the slave or draw pictures that show what the slave's life was like.

6. For a better idea of what the holidays were like on a plantation, read from *Christmas in the Big House, Christmas in the Quarters* with students. (See page 78 for more information.) Compare and contrast the differences in holiday preparations and celebrations between the planter's family and the families of slaves on a plantation.

A HOME IN THE SLAVE QUARTERS

Houses in the slave quarters were different on different plantations. But, few of them had even common comforts to offer. A slave cabin at Thomas Jefferson's estate, Monticello, was typical of those found on many plantations: 14' x 12' (4.25 m x 3.65 m) with a dirt floor and a fireplace. Many slave quarter homes had no windows. Often, there was one large bed, usually attached to a wall to save lumber. Favored slaves might have a two-room house, but this was rare. Whole families lived and slept in these tiny homes with very few possessions.

This activity will help students explore the life of a plantation slave from the perspective of a basic human experience: the experience of home.

FOLLOW THESE STEPS:

1. First, read the following text aloud to students:

Read →

The master of a plantation usually gave the same things to each slave family. It was not very much. Most slave cabins had one big bed. This bed was attached to a wall. That saved wood for the legs, but it meant that the bed could not be moved. The slave family also had only one blanket to share.

Most slave homes had a fireplace. That was good because the family could use it for heat and for cooking food. The master gave each family one big iron pot for cooking. They also were given one cooking spoon. Sometimes, a slave family was also given a little grinder, or mill. This was used for grinding dried corn to make cornmeal.

Think about living in a house that only had one big bed and one cooking pot. What else would you need so that your family could eat, live, and sleep in the house?

Remember, slaves did not have money to buy things. If they stole things, they would be punished. Everything else they had in their homes they either made or received as a gift.

2. Distribute copies of the reproducibles on pages 20 and 21. First, have students complete the Student Activity Questions on page 20. This will help them think about the difficulties of furnishing a slave house and making it comfortable. Then, have each student complete the drawing of her cabin in the slave quarters by adding details to the diagram on page 21.

3. After students have completed their worksheets, have small groups or the whole class discuss the problems that slaves might have faced trying to find and make things for their families' homes. What things do students think were most important? Why?

4. Discuss some ways that slaves with different talents could have worked together to furnish their cabins. For example, a slave who was good with wood could make chairs from scrap lumber or tree branches, or a slave who knew how to sew could save scraps of material and make quilts.

PLANTATION LIFE

STUDENT READING PASSAGE

DIRECTIONS: Read the story. Then, answer the questions.

Slaves lived in cities, in towns, and on farms. They lived in both the North and the South. But over time, Northern states made owning slaves against the law. Many slaves lived together on large farms called **plantations**. Many of these plantations were in the South.

Life on a plantation was hard. There were two groups of slaves. The slaves in one group were called **house slaves**. These slaves worked in the big house of the owner, or **master**, of a plantation. They cooked, sewed, and cleaned. They served the owner and his family. Slave women sometimes took care of the owner's children and could not take care of their own children. Sometimes, house slaves lived in small rooms in the master's house. Other times, they lived in the **slave quarters**. This was a group of tiny shacks on a plantation. Each family lived in one of the little houses.

The other group of slaves were called **field hands**. These slaves worked on the farm. They planted and harvested crops. They fixed fences and fed farm animals. They worked long hours in the hot sun. In many ways, their work was harder than the work of the house slaves.

All slaves lived in the shadow of the master of a plantation. The master ruled life on his plantation. Some masters let their slaves learn to read and write. Some masters gave their slaves enough to eat. Other masters were cruel. They made life very hard. All masters could choose to sell slaves to work on other farms, just like they could sell horses or cows. A slave child could be sold to another plantation. The child's mother and father might never see him or her again. Parents were sold, too. These things made life terrible and sad for slaves.

Name: _____ Date: _____

DIRECTIONS: Circle the correct answers.

1. What did a **house slave** do?

   a. worked in the fields
   b. cooked and cleaned
   c. took care of the master's children
   d. b. and c.

2. A **field hand** was—

   a. a slave who worked in the big house.
   b. a slave who cooked for the master's family.
   c. a slave who was in charge of a plantation.
   d. none of the above

DIRECTIONS: Write a short answer.

3. If you were a slave, would you rather have worked in the fields or the house? Why?

   _____

   _____

DIRECTIONS: Write T for true and F for false.

4. _____ All black people lived on **plantations**.

5. _____ No slaves learned to read or write.

6. _____ **Plantations** were large farms owned by slaves.

7. _____ The shacks, or small houses, where slaves lived were called the **slave quarters**.

DIRECTIONS: Answer the questions in complete sentences.

8. What do you think was the hardest thing about being a slave? Why? _____

   _____

   _____

   _____

UNIT 2: LIFE ON A PLANTATION

THE MASTER'S DIARY

STUDENT ACTIVITY

DIRECTIONS: Read the diary entries. Then, discuss them with your class.

The Master's Diary

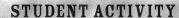

June 27—I am going to sell Hector. My neighbor, John Jones, wants to buy him. This was a hard choice, but my son, James, needs his own riding horse. Selling Hector is the best way to raise the money. Hector is married to Betty, my cook. She will be unhappy with my choice. But, John Jones lives only five miles from here. I will tell Betty that she can see Hector one day every year at Christmas.

September 12—The harvest is over. The holidays will be here soon. My daughter, Emily, wants her own maid. She says that she will be going to other homes for holiday visits. All of her friends bring their own maids to these visits. So, I am going to move my slave, Phoebe, out of the fields and into the house. Phoebe is about 12 years old now. She will not see very much of her mother or her brothers and sisters after the move. But, Phoebe does not seem very strong. One day she fainted in the fields. Emily says she will train Phoebe to be a lady's maid.

November 12—My slave, Jupiter, who was serving in the house, has run away. I have hired a man to go after him. Jupiter will be caught and brought back to my plantation. When Jupiter is found, I will put him to work in the fields. I will make sure he gets the hardest jobs. This will teach him not to run away again.

December 1—My wife told me today that I need to choose holiday gifts for the slaves. It looks like it will be a hard, cold winter. So, I think I will give each family a new blanket. This, along with the food to make their holiday dinners, is more than enough for the slaves as a group. I also want to give new clothes and a coat to my slave, Jesse. He is my manservant. He needs better-looking clothes. The other slaves might not like it that Jesse will get more, but that is not important. My wife seems happy with my choices.

Name: _____ Date: _____

DIRECTIONS: Look at the diagram on page 21. Read the description. Then, answer the questions.

1. How many beds will you need for your family? (Remember: many slave children shared beds.)

    _____

    How could you make more beds? _____

    _____

2. What other things do you think you might need for cooking and eating?

    _____

    _____

    What could you make or trade for these things? _____

    _____

3. Is there room for more furniture in your cabin? _____

    If you answered yes, what kind of furniture do you want to add? _____

    _____

    _____

    What will you make or trade for this additional furniture? _____

    _____

    _____

4. Do you think it will be nice to live in your cabin? Why or why not? _____

    _____

    _____

    _____

    _____

UNIT 2: LIFE ON A PLANTATION

A HOME IN THE SLAVE QUARTERS

STUDENT ACTIVITY

DIRECTIONS: Look at the diagram and read the description. Answer the questions on the worksheet on page 20. Then, use this page to draw and plan things to add to your cabin.

This is a one-room house in the slave quarters. It has a fireplace. There is one bed. It is built in and cannot be moved. There are no windows. There is one door. This is where you will live with your mother, father, two brothers, and one sister. This view shows your house looking down from the ceiling.

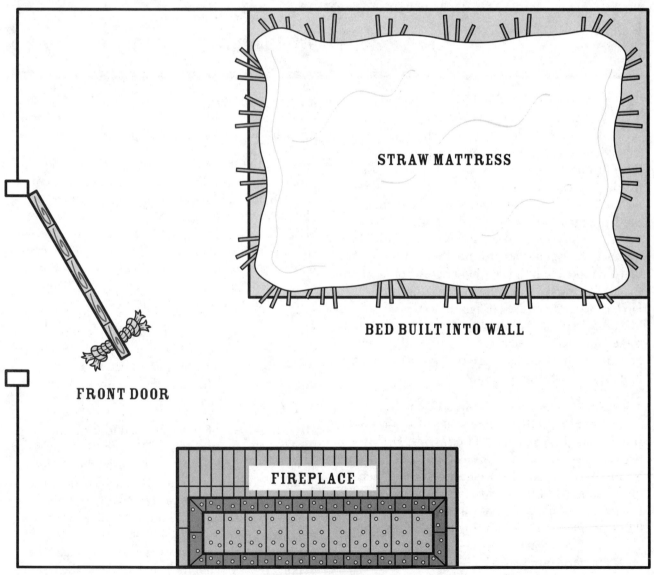

STRAW MATTRESS

BED BUILT INTO WALL

FRONT DOOR

FIREPLACE

**14 FEET X 12 FEET
(4.25 METERS X 3.65 METERS)**

When the first Fugitive Slave Act passed in 1793, a citizen of the United States could no longer legally stand in the way of someone trying to capture a runaway slave. Ironically, it was probably the passing of this law that helped to solidify a growing, secret network of help for runaway slaves, later called the Underground Railroad. Historians estimate that the first organized Underground Railroad routes were established around 1800, although by that time people had been helping escaping slaves for 200 years. By 1860, the northern part of the United States from New England to the upper Midwest was a web of safe houses and supervised routes for escaping slaves. There were also participants in the South, where this work was even more dangerous and difficult.

The term "Underground Railroad" may have been coined in 1831 by the master of a successfully escaped slave named Tice Davids. Davids heroically swam the dangerous Ohio River to escape from his closely pursuing master. When the master rowed to the far side of the riverbank, Davids was gone, probably carried away by free black people who were waiting there to help him. The mystified owner said, "He must have gone on an underground road."

The language of the Underground Railroad employed the railway metaphor. A *conductor* was a person who helped slaves travel from one place to the next. A *station* was a safe house. An escaping slave was called a *passenger*.

How did the slaves find help through the Underground Railroad? They used an amazing system of codes. Some field hands sang songs that were actually messages and instructions for how to escape. Slaves sometimes made quilts that contained pictorial "maps" and information for escape. Conductors marked safe paths by making cuts in tree bark or using piled stones, and they marked safe houses with strategically placed candles or lanterns.

Escaping slaves usually traveled at night since they were less likely to be detected and caught under the cover of darkness. They had to walk huge distances. The journey usually took a year or more to complete.

Many hundreds of people helped to form the Underground Railroad even though they all risked arrest. Thousands of slaves who used the Underground Railroad were even braver because if they were captured, they would be severely punished or sold away from their families. One of the most famous conductors, a former slave named Harriet Tubman, even risked losing her own freedom by making 19 trips into the South to help other escaping slaves travel north.

One way slaves helped each other use the Underground Railroad was through coded songs. Today, we know that songs, such as "Steal Away" and "Wade in the Water," were coded, but we can only guess their specific meanings. That is because the meaning had to be cleverly hidden so that overseers and other white people who heard the songs could not understand the embedded directions. We have the most information about a song called "Follow the Drinking Gourd." In this activity, students will learn more about the song and then try to compose lyrics to their own secret songs.

FOLLOW THESE STEPS:

1. Read the text of the first two stanzas of "Follow the Drinking Gourd" aloud. Discuss the possible explanations of the code that follow each stanza with students.

2. Ask students to choose a place they all know well, such as the school playground, a park, or the block around the school building. How would students use codes to tell someone how to get there? Select a site. Make copies of the reproducible on page 27 to help students identify landmarks and directions around the chosen site. After students have finished their worksheets individually, use these ideas and work together to compose lyrics in code to describe and give directions to the selected place.

When the sun comes back
And the first quail calls,
Follow the drinking gourd.
For the old man is a-waiting for to
carry you to freedom
If you follow the drinking gourd.

Meaning: Many people believe that the "old man" was a carpenter called Peg Leg Joe, a conductor on the Underground Railroad. In the first stanza, slaves are told to start an escape during the winter when the quails migrate to the South. It would take a slave from Mississippi or Alabama about one year to get to the Ohio River—the boundary between the South and the North. Because the Ohio River was so wide, it was better to cross it when it was frozen. A slave starting in winter would arrive at the Ohio River at the correct time. The "drinking gourd" refers to the Big Dipper. This constellation points to the North Star and was a slave's best guide to freedom.

The riverbank makes a very good road,
The dead trees show you the way.
Left foot, peg foot, traveling on,
Follow the drinking gourd.

Meaning: This stanza is directing slaves to follow a river north, a river that passes through a wetland area with many dead trees lining it. It may have been referring to the Tombigbee River in Alabama. The "left foot, peg foot" portion probably alludes to special trailblazing marks left by Peg Leg Joe on the trees. Every stanza of the song reminds slaves to use the Big Dipper to keep them on a northward path.

This activity will introduce students to just some of the dangers and difficulties that slaves faced as they planned their escape to freedom in the North. Although the Underground Railroad network existed to help escaping slaves, many of them had to make the journey through the deep South on their own.

Perhaps the most dangerous part of a slave's journey to freedom was at the beginning: escaping from the plantation and traveling over nearby land. Not only did a slave have a better chance of being recognized close to home, but it was also more likely that his owner or others from the plantation were searching for him there. Slaves had a poor chance of getting a good head start since it would probably not be long before someone noticed that they had left. Slaves who took items with them could be accused of stealing, as well as escaping, if they were caught.

As slaves journeyed to unfamiliar ground, they faced different risks. Perhaps a safe house, or station, was no longer safe—some owners of stations actually turned in slaves for rewards. Perhaps a farm had a vicious dog, or woods that looked safe were set with hunting traps. Rivers might have strong currents and be difficult to cross. Without guns or knives, slaves could not hunt for food and instead had to forage in fields and woods. All of these things added to their difficulties.

When slaves finally made it to an Underground Railroad route, they were still in danger. But, at least these routes offered guides, safe places to sleep, meals, and sometimes baths and clean clothes.

FOLLOW THESE STEPS:

1. Make copies of the map on page 28 for students. Explain that this map shows part of one day's journey for an escaping group of slaves. This is an area not far from the slaves' plantation. The information on the map represents things their group knows about the surrounding countryside and houses. They will also need the following information:

☞ A cousin of one of the slaves in your group works in the kitchen next to the plantation house.

☞ There are cooked hams and turkeys in the plantation smokehouse.

☞ Slave hunters often gather at trading posts.

☞ There is a loud dog outside of the trading post.

☞ Your group isn't sure if the small cabin across the river from the church is empty.

☞ The church is usually empty during the week.

☞ Miss Smith is known for helping escaped slaves.

☞ There is another loud dog outside of the Jones's farmhouse.

☞ There are no slaves at Cooper's Chicken Farm, but the owner has helped catch runaway slaves before.

☞ Men sometimes hunt at night in the Middle Woods.

2. Tell students that they will pretend to be escaping slaves traveling in groups of four. Then, divide students into groups. Ask each group to study the map. They need to work together to choose a way to cross the area pictured on the map. They must reach an agreement about which way to go. During the escape, members of the group must stay together the whole time.

3. Give students copies of the reproducible on page 29. Have them answer the questions as a group. Again, they must agree on their answers. With younger students, you may want to circulate and give input as they work with the map and worksheet.

4. Bring the entire class together. Ask each group to make a presentation about their escape route. Make sure that each group explains why they made the choices they did. Then, as a class, vote about which escape route would be the safest.

ESCAPE!

STUDENT READING PASSAGE

DIRECTIONS: Read the story. Then, answer the questions.

What was the **Underground Railroad**? It wasn't a real railroad at all. It was a group of people who worked together to help slaves escape to freedom in the North. These people, in both the North and the South, helped slaves go from one safe place to another. Some of the people built houses with secret hiding places for the slaves. Some of them marked paths that showed safe ways around farms or across rivers. These people were called **conductors**. They knew that helping slaves run away was against the law. But, they thought the law was wrong.

The brave slaves helped each other, too. They made up songs to sing while they worked in the fields. These songs used codes to tell of paths that slaves could use to escape. Some slaves made quilts. The quilts looked like they had pictures on them. But, the pictures were really secret maps.

In many cases, the Underground Railroad started in places close to the North. Slaves had to find their own way to the first **station**, or safe house. They used the songs and quilts to help them find their way. They also had to make many hard choices about which way to go. They had to pick ways to get to places where people would help them.

One slave who escaped to freedom in the North went back to help other slaves. Her name was Harriet Tubman. This amazing woman made 19 trips back into the South. She helped more than 300 people escape from slavery. If she had been caught, she would have been sent back into slavery herself. Slaves who were caught were also whipped. Sometimes, they were sold and sent to other plantations away from their families. Even with all of the danger, many brave people worked together to make the "railroad" run.

Name: _____ Date: _____

DIRECTIONS: Circle the correct answers.

1. The **Underground Railroad** was—

   a. a secret way to help slaves escape.
   b. a train that went from the North to the South.
   c. a group of people who worked together to hide slaves and help them.
   d. a. and c.

2. A **conductor** was—

   a. a person who was running away from slavery.
   b. a person who had been caught and taken back to slavery.
   c. a person who marked paths or made hiding places for runaway slaves.
   d. a person who caught runaway slaves.

3. A **station** was—

   a. a plantation with slaves.
   b. a safe house where escaping slaves could hide.
   c. a place where escaping slaves could catch trains.
   d. none of the above

DIRECTIONS: Write T for true and F for false.

4. _____ It was against the law to help slaves run away from their masters.

5. _____ Harriet Tubman was caught and sent back to slavery.

6. _____ Slaves who were caught running away were punished.

7. _____ Slaves sometimes made quilts that were really secret maps to freedom.

DIRECTIONS: Answer the question in complete sentences.

8. What was one way that people in the Underground Railroad helped slaves escape?

   _____

   _____

   _____

   _____

UNIT 3: ESCAPING SLAVERY

STEAL AWAY

STUDENT ACTIVITY QUESTIONS

DIRECTIONS: Answer the questions to help you write a coded slave song.

1. We are going to write a song about how to get from _____
   _____ to _____ .

2. Draw a small map of the route your class has chosen.

3. What landmarks are along this route? What stands out? Is there a special tree? Is there a statue? Is there a sign of some kind? List three landmarks.

   a. _____

   b. _____

   c. _____

4. The person using your song must be able to see each landmark and understand your descriptions. But, a slave owner or overseer listening to the song must not be able to tell what you are singing about. How could you tell about each landmark in a secret way?

   a. _____

   b. _____

   c. _____

5. Name one other thing that you think you need to say in your song.

   _____

UNIT 3: ESCAPING SLAVERY
PLAN YOUR ESCAPE
STUDENT ACTIVITY

This map shows part of your journey to freedom. You are trying to get to Miss Smith's house. She will hide you for the night. Study the map carefully. Then, use the questions on page 29 to help you make choices about your trip. It is about 6 o'clock in the evening when you start. It is just starting to get dark.

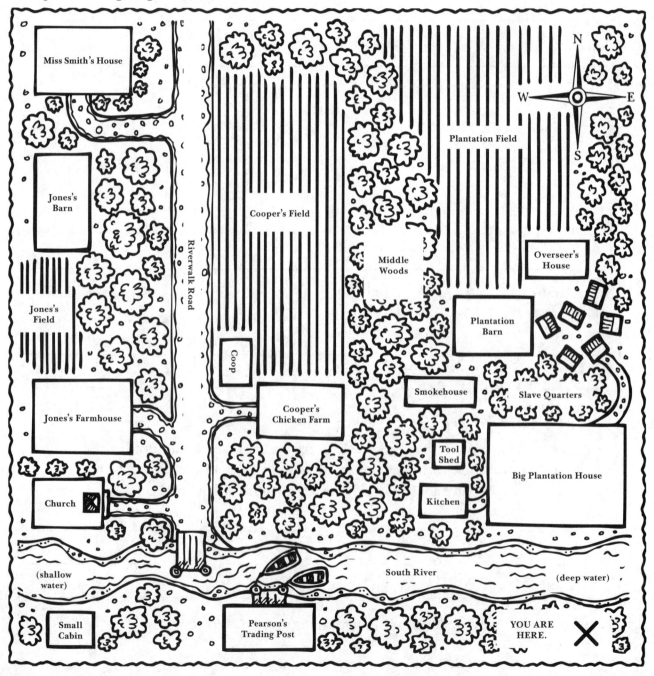

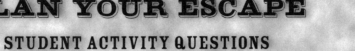

UNIT 3: ESCAPING SLAVERY

PLAN YOUR ESCAPE

STUDENT ACTIVITY QUESTIONS

DIRECTIONS: Use the map on page 28 to answer the following questions about your escape plan.

1. Where will you cross the river? Why? _____

   _____

2. Will you try to take a boat?   **YES**   **NO**

   Why or why not? _____

   _____

3. Once you are across the river, where will you go next? Why? _____

   _____

   _____

4. What are the main dangers you will face along the way? List three dangers.

   a._____

   b._____

   c. _____

5. Where are three places that you might find food?

   a._____

   b._____

   c. _____

   Which place to find food is the safest? Why? _____

   _____

6. Name three safe places where you could hide.

   a._____

   b._____

   c. _____

The abolitionist movement in the United States had deep roots. Early abolitionists included many members of the Society of Friends (the Quakers) who performed brave acts of civil disobedience against slave owners as early as the colonial period. Later, they helped solidify aid to escaping slaves through the Underground Railroad. Another outspoken protester of slavery was William Lloyd Garrison, the publisher of a weekly newspaper called the *Liberator*. The author Harriet Beecher Stowe, in publishing *Uncle Tom's Cabin*, caught the imagination of thousands of people who read her novel with its graphic descriptions of life on a plantation and the perils of escape.

Although many well-known abolitionists were white, many African Americans also threw themselves into this work and were leaders and motivators who helped shift public opinion. Early abolition leaders included David Walker, who courageously attempted to speak directly to slaves in the South through his antislavery book, *Appeal to the Coloured Citizens of the World*. Walker urged slaves to rise up against slavery and their masters. In fact, his outspoken work may have been the reason for his mysterious death in 1830. Maria Stewart, a follower of Walker, became both an abolitionist speaker and an early promoter of equal rights for women. Frederick Douglass, an escaped slave, was an author and speaker, and he was the publisher of the *North Star*, another weekly newspaper for the cause. Sojourner Truth, one of the most famous voices to speak against slavery, was a powerful orator and personal witness to the cruel treatment that slaves suffered.

The abolitionist movement worked tirelessly until the eve of the Civil War. The leaders of the movement were adept at using available media to present their cause. Slave narratives—stories told by escaped slaves—were popular publications. Weekly newspapers told of political battles and the most recent news concerning slavery laws and opposition. Public speeches by escaped slaves and famous orators urged people to rise up against slavery and demand its end.

Within the movement, there was some disagreement about tactics to bring about the end of slavery. Some felt that it could be accomplished through peaceful means—a gradual shifting of the laws. Others, such as Garrison and Douglass, felt that there must be no delay in doing all that could be done and that a war was inevitable. Regardless of opposing views among abolitionists, their combined work did contribute to the ultimate realization of their goal: abolishing slavery in the United States of America.

By the mid-19th century, there was a marked difference in the treatment of African Americans in the North as compared to the South. Although African Americans did not face ideal or even acceptable treatment in the North, they did live in freedom. They could work for a living and be paid for their work. In the South, slaves were strictly property. They were bought and sold as commodities.

There are few documents that underscore these differences as well as newspaper clippings of the time. Advertisements for runaway slaves became commonplace, and many of those ads show us that slaves were running away to try to reconnect with family members lost through slave sales. Slaves were described by color as if they were animals. On the other hand, in Northern newspapers, advertisements and articles describing speakers for the abolition movement depicted African Americans as interesting people with something to say. In this exercise, students will explore these differences.

Note: In order to maintain grade-level readability, the two examples on page 35 are not primary documents; they were written for this exercise.

FOLLOW THESE STEPS:

1. Distribute copies of the reproducible on page 35. With younger students, read the selections aloud as they follow along.

2. Use these questions to start a class discussion.

☞ Which newspaper piece is from the North? Which piece is from the South? How can you tell?

☞ What is the purpose of the first piece?

☞ What is the purpose of the second piece?

☞ **What is the same about the two pieces?** They both are about the same person, Tobias Smith; they are both about someone escaping from slavery; they both describe some of the same events.

☞ **What makes the two pieces different?** One is an advertisement and the other is a newspaper article. The plantation owner describes Tobias as a "boy" even though he is 30 years old and says that he bought Tobias; the plantation owner thinks Tobias is his property and wants Tobias returned or taken to jail. The newspaper article talks about Tobias Smith, a person—someone who is working, is smart, and was brave to escape.

☞ **What else do you notice about the two pieces?** You might discuss the concept of offering a reward, Tobias's new job at the *North Star* and why this newspaper would be a good place for him to work, etc.

☞ **What kinds of things do you think Tobias might talk about in his speech?** Discuss details from other units, such as what a slave's life was like and what it might have been like for Tobias and Maria to be separated.

Public speeches were a very effective medium for abolitionists. In Northern cities, antislavery speeches were popular and well attended. Sometimes, a white abolitionist or writer would speak. These speeches helped people form political opinions about the abolishment of slavery. At other times, speeches would be made by African Americans who had escaped from slavery and told about the miseries of their lives and the dangers of escaping. These first-hand accounts helped people understand what slaves endured on an emotional level.

In this activity, students will write brief antislavery speeches after listening to and discussing quotations from famous abolitionists.

FOLLOW THESE STEPS:

1. Read a selection of quotations from abolitionist speeches to students. Use the quotations below or create your own collection. Read each quotation and then ask students to paraphrase it. This will help them understand its meaning in their own words.

> *"I didn't know I was a slave until I found out I couldn't do the things I wanted."*
>
> **—Frederick Douglass**

> *"The white man's happiness cannot be purchased by the black man's misery."*
>
> **—Frederick Douglass**

> *"[On the subject of freeing the slaves]—I will not retreat a single inch—AND I WILL BE HEARD."*
>
> **—William Lloyd Garrison**

> *"When you get into a tight place and everything goes against you, till it seems you could not hold on a minute longer, never give up then, for that is just the place and time that the tide will turn."*
>
> **—Harriet Beecher Stowe**

> *"The greatest riches in all America have arisen from our blood and tears."*
>
> **—David Walker**

2. Distribute copies of the reproducible on page 36. Ask students to complete the worksheet individually or in small groups.

3. Make copies of the reproducible on page 37 to help students write antislavery speeches. For younger students, these speeches can be as short as three sentences—one for the introduction, one for the body, and one for the conclusion.

4. Have students present their speeches to the class.

DIRECTIONS: Read the story. Then, answer the questions.

Slave owners did not think there was anything wrong with owning slaves. They thought of slaves as **property**, something they owned. They did not think of slaves as people. There were also many people who thought slavery was wrong. They wanted to make it against the law. These people were called **abolitionists**. Many of these people helped run the Underground Railroad. They also had another important job. They spoke out against slavery. They helped people see that slavery was wrong.

The abolitionists did not have televisions, the Internet, or radios. So, how did they get other people to listen to them? They used newspapers. Some people even started their own newspapers to talk about the evils of slavery. They also wrote books. Former slaves wrote about their lives and their escapes from the South. Abolitionists also gave speeches. People would come to hear famous abolitionists speak. Escaped slaves also made speeches.

Many of the people who spoke against slavery are still famous today. One was Frederick Douglass. He was a slave until he ran away. He wrote a book about his life. He made many speeches, too. He also ran a newspaper called the *North Star*.

Sojourner Truth was another famous speaker. She had been a slave. She talked about rights for slaves and for women. She asked the people who listened to her, "Ain't I a woman?" She might have meant, "Look at what I can do! I am as strong as a man. I am a woman, but I do not get special treatment like white women do. I have to be strong."

Not long before the Civil War, a famous book about slavery was published. The book was ***Uncle Tom's Cabin***. It was about the hard lives of slaves. The author was Harriet Beecher Stowe. Her story was read by thousands of people at the time. It helped change many people's minds about slavery.

UNIT 4: ABOLITION

SPEAKING OUT

STUDENT READING QUESTIONS

DIRECTIONS: Circle the correct answers.

1. The **abolitionists** were—

   a. owners of slaves.
   b. people who created a television show.
   c. people who spoke out against slavery.
   d. none of the above

2. *Uncle Tom's Cabin* was—

   a. a famous speech.
   b. a book by Harriet Beecher Stowe.
   c. a book that told about the terrible lives of slaves.
   d. b. and c.

3. One famous person who spoke against slavery was—

   a. Sojourner Douglass.
   b. Harriet Truth.
   c. Frederick Stowe.
   d. none of the above

DIRECTIONS: Write T for true and F for false.

4. _____ **Property** means "things someone owns."

5. _____ The abolitionists gave speeches on television to get their message heard.

6. _____ Frederick Douglass was a white man.

7. _____ One abolitionist newspaper was called the *North Star*.

DIRECTIONS: Answer the question in complete sentences.

8. How did abolitionists and former slaves tell other people about the wrongs of slavery? Describe the ways they spread their messages.

_____

_____

_____

_____

DIRECTIONS: Read the passages. Then, discuss them with your class.

RUNAWAY SLAVE! $100 REWARD

My boy, Tobias, ran off about three weeks ago. I bought him from the Kingsbury Plantation on the River Charles. He had a wife there. He may be going there to see her. He is about 30 years of age. He is a dark brown color. He has a scar on his left cheek. He is about six feet tall. He was wearing a dark blue jacket, blue pants, and brown boots. If you catch him, deliver him to me at River Plantation in Charles County, Virginia, or take him to the Charles County jail.

Signed, *Thomas Lake*

A STORY OF ESCAPE!

ESCAPED SLAVE TO GIVE SPEECH ON THE HORRORS OF SLAVERY

Tonight, Mr. Tobias Smith, formerly of Virginia, will describe how he ran away from a cruel master named Thomas Lake. Mr. Smith will speak in the Franklin Theater. The speech is free and open to the public.

Mr. Smith ran away from a plantation on January 2, 1851. He spent three weeks in hiding. He could hear people in the woods looking for him. He kept away from them, hiding in the woods and in a secret cave. Then, he went to the Kingsbury Plantation where his wife, Maria, was working. Thomas Lake had bought Mr. Smith there but would not let Mr. and Mrs. Smith stay together. Mr. Smith was able to help his wife escape, too.

Tobias and Maria Smith spent six months running from danger. They came here to Boston. Mr. Smith will speak about the horrors of his life as a slave. Do not miss this powerful speech!

Mr. Smith now works as a writer for this newspaper, the *North Star*, the voice of FREEDOM.

UNIT 4: ABOLITION

POWERFUL WORDS

STUDENT ACTIVITY QUESTIONS

Imagine you are going to give a speech against slavery. Answer the questions to help you plan your speech.

DIRECTIONS: Circle your choices.

1. You are going to pretend to be—

   a. an escaped slave.

   b. a writer for a newspaper.

   c. a politician.

2. You are going to write your speech about—

   a. the terrible lives of slaves.

   b. your belief that the laws must change.

   c. your own feelings about slavery.

3. You would like the people who hear your speech to *mostly* feel—

   a. angry about slavery.

   b. sad about the slaves in the South.

   c. happy for the slaves who have escaped.

   d. sure that they should speak out about the wrongs of slavery.

DIRECTIONS: Finish each sentence as if you are giving your speech.

4. The main reason I am making a speech about slavery is _____

   _____

   _____ .

5. I have spoken about slavery _____ times before.

6. One detail I will use in my speech is _____

   _____

   _____

   _____ .

Name: _____ Date: _____

DIRECTIONS: Use the organizer to plan your speech. Then, write your speech.

TITLE: The title of my speech is

PLACE: I will deliver my speech at Franklin Hall in Boston, Massachusetts.

INTRODUCTION: Get people to listen by making a strong opening statement.

BODY: Tell about the problem. Give examples so that people will know your point of view is true. Give details that people will remember.

CONCLUSION: Tell people what you would like them to do.

The time leading up to the Civil War was one of the most difficult periods in American history. The country was essentially split in half in regards to both the economy and slavery. The North was highly industrialized, and the Missouri Compromise confirmed all Northern states as free states. The abolitionist movement in the North was highly vocal and received a great deal of coverage in Northern newspapers. But, not everyone in the North was against slavery. The North simply was not dependent economically on the institution of slavery.

In the South, the actual percentage of slave owners was low. But, large plantations with cash crops demanded big labor forces. Rich planters benefited for years from a labor force that they did not have to pay: slaves. However, competition for slaves had become intense since 1808. That was the year the federal government made it illegal to bring slaves from Africa. This raised the monetary value of slaves already in the United States, and the prices continued to escalate. By 1858, one acre of land might sell for $15; a single slave could be worth as much as $1,000. Because of these rising values, plantation owners were more determined than ever to pursue African Americans who tried to escape from slavery.

In the years just before the Civil War, changes to the law made this tragic transformation even more brutal. The Fugitive Slave Act of 1850, a part of the Compromise of 1850, made it possible for slave hunters to enter the North to take escaped slaves back to the South without warrants. Some free black people were taken illegally into slavery because of this law. Anyone helping a fugitive slave would face jail or be fined $1,000—a staggering amount of money at the time. Only Canada was safe for African Americans fleeing from slavery.

The Dred Scott decision of 1857 ruled that Congress could not ban slavery in the western territories, overturning the Missouri Compromise. Even worse, the decision stated that no African American, not even a free black person, could ever be a citizen. Because of this, Dred Scott did not even have the right to bring his case to court—something that African Americans had been doing since the 17th century. Laws like these made in the 1850s eventually helped to propel the divided country into war, even though the focus of secession was on states' rights and the economy rather than slavery itself.

When the Fugitive Slave Act of 1850 was passed, African Americans who were living in Northern states were suddenly at risk. The act's provisions allowed black people under suspicion as escaped slaves to be taken without a warrant. Slave hunters started going into Northern states to look for black people under suspicion of being escaped slaves, and it was against the law to stand in their way. In 1850 alone, several thousand African Americans who had been living in Northern states moved to Canada. In 1858, after the Dred Scott decision, more African Americans fled to Canada because of a new law that said that the United States viewed them as property even if they had been born free. Slaves who escaped during this time knew they had to make their way to the Canadian border to reach safety.

Why Canada? Canada was ruled by British law, and Great Britain had strict laws against slavery. Great Britain stood firm in its antislavery stance. Ultimately, the British would not aid the South in the Civil War, even though they needed Southern cotton for their cloth mills.

FOLLOW THESE STEPS:

1. Talk to students about the changing laws in the mid-19th century that made Canada an appealing place. Use these discussion questions to help students focus on African Americans' feelings about the changing laws:

☞ What would it be like to suddenly feel unsafe in a place that you thought was safe?

☞ Imagine you are a free black person living in the North, but your wife or husband is an escaped slave. How would the new laws change your life?

☞ Would it be hard to leave your home? What things do you think African Americans missed about their homes in the United States?

2. Next, tell students that there is a song that shows how some African Americans felt about going to Canada. This song was about escaping slaves, not black people already living in the North.

3. Make copies of the reproducible on page 44. Have students read the song lyrics to themselves, or read them together as a class. Students may need help with some of the words and their meanings. Review some of the vocabulary and ideas. For example:

☞ What does *dreary* mean?

☞ What does *resolved* mean?

☞ What are the "baying hounds" described in the song? What's happening in this part?

☞ Who is Queen Victoria? Why are her arms "held wide"? What does this mean?

☞ What do these words tell you about the various feelings in the song?

4. Sing the song to the tune of "O, Susannah!"

Note: The original version of "I'm on My Way to Canada" has been edited to better suit this activity.

Starting in 1850, the emotional landscape of the United States changed for both African Americans and abolitionists. The Fugitive Slave Act took away the security that the North provided for many who had escaped from slavery. Even those who had escaped slavery as small children and lived most of their lives as participants in a free society were at risk to be captured and returned to slavery. Bounty hunters became aggressive in the wake of this law and freely entered Northern states to search for former slaves.

Help students try to understand what it felt like to live in this era by playing this simple game.

FOLLOW THESE STEPS:

1. Select a site with plenty of room to run. If you can clear a space in the classroom and your school will tolerate the noise, students can play this game inside. If your school has a playground, play outside.

2. Designate a small area at one end of the site as the "safe zone." This could be the area around your desk or the steps of a playground area. Be sure there is a clear line or boundary that divides the safe zone from the rest of the site.

3. Divide the class into three groups: runners, helpers, and catchers.

☞ Approximately five percent of students should be helpers. Give each helper a small piece of paper to carry with an *H* written on it. These students start out in the safe zone. Their job is to leave the safe zone and try to help other people get to the safe zone—by getting catchers to chase them instead of runners or by other means of distraction. If they are caught, however, they can show their pieces of paper and return to the safe zone.

☞ Designate approximately 10 percent of students as catchers. It is their job to tag anyone who is trying to get to the safe zone and escort them to the opposite end of the site.

☞ The remaining students will be runners. It is their job to try to get from the unsafe area to the safe zone. Tell runners that once they are in the safe zone, they can choose to go back and help others. Unlike helpers, if they are caught, they cannot go back to the safe zone. They must go back to the opposite end of the site and try to reach the safe zone again.

☞ For the helpers and runners, the object of the game is to get as many people into the safe zone as possible.

4. After play has gone on for a while, clap your hands and tell everyone to freeze in position. Announce that there is no longer a safe zone. Runners will have to keep running to stay away from catchers; they have nowhere to go to rest. Allow this to continue for a short time before calling an end to the game. Then, discuss the meaning of the game in terms of the changing laws and escaping slaves. What must it have felt like when there was no longer a "safe zone" within the United States?

Note: This game should be played like "tag." Catchers may not use force to keep runners away from the safe zone.

DRED SCOTT: PERSON OR PROPERTY?

One of the harshest parts of the Dred Scott decision was the Supreme Court's ruling about citizenship. The ruling stated that no one of African ancestry could be considered a citizen of the United States. This even applied to black people who were born free and lived in the North. The ruling made it clear that Dred Scott, as an African American, had no right to sue in court since that right was reserved for citizens of the United States. The decision also took all citizenship rights from the entire body of African Americans in the United States.

This activity will help students understand the consequences of this decision, which was later overturned by an amendment to the Constitution.

FOLLOW THESE STEPS:

1. Discuss the following questions:

☞ **What does it mean to be a citizen?**
    You are a member of a society; you have rights that are protected.

☞ **In the United States, how are a citizen's rights protected?**
    The Constitution and the court system protect citizens' rights.

☞ **What rights do U.S. citizens have?**
    U.S. citizens have the right to vote, the right to live and speak freely, the right to go to court to fix problems, the right to refuse to have their homes searched without warrants, the right to practice any religion, etc.

2. Talk about the lives of black people in the North just before the Civil War. Although they could not vote, they did live in communities as members of society. They had jobs, they went to church, and they had homes and families. They used the courts to resolve issues. Some black people ran newspapers where they gave their opinions about slavery and other issues. Some of these people were escaped slaves, and others were free from birth. Talk about how African Americans used the rights of citizenship in their everyday lives.

3. Explain to students how the Dred Scott decision changed the lives of thousands of African Americans in the North. You may want to give additional background about the Dred Scott case: who he was, why he was suing in court, etc.

4. Distribute copies of the reproducible on page 45. Divide students into small groups so that they can use the worksheet and discuss the answers at the same time. Have students work together to answer the questions.

DIRECTIONS: Read the story. Then, answer the questions.

By the middle of the 1800s, the situation in the United States was bad. The North and the South saw things very differently. Part of the reason for this was the way people worked and made money.

In the North, most people worked on small farms or in factories. They did not need big groups of workers to run these places.

In the South, some people had big plantations. These people needed lots of workers for their huge fields of crops. Over time, they grew accustomed to having slaves work these jobs. They did not have to pay slaves. This helped them make even more money when they sold their crops.

The government would not let people bring more slaves from Africa. So, slaves in the United States were worth a large amount of money. They were worth even more than the farmland.

Plantation owners in the South tried harder than ever to keep slaves from running away. They helped push new laws that made it more difficult for slaves to run away. One law said that anybody helping a slave escape would be fined $1,000! Another law said that slaves were not free just because they ran away to free states. This meant that to be safe from slave hunters, slaves had to get to Canada because slavery was illegal there.

The new laws made many people angry. Many people in the North felt that slavery was wrong. In the South, some people felt that slaves were necessary. The two sides could not agree. There was no **middle ground**.

UNIT 5: THE WIDENING GAP
TWO SIDES, NO MIDDLE
STUDENT READING QUESTIONS

DIRECTIONS: Circle the correct answers.

1. Many people in the South felt that—

    a. slaves were needed to work in factories.

    b. slaves were needed to work on plantations.

    c. slavery was wrong.

    d. none of the above

2. In the North, many people worked—

    a. on large farms called plantations.

    b. on boats.

    c. in cotton fields.

    d. on small farms and in factories.

3. "There was no **middle ground**" means—

    a. there was no land between the North and the South.

    b. there was no middle view, just two arguing sides.

    c. there was no ground to stand on.

    d. there was only one side.

DIRECTIONS: Fill in each blank with the correct word.

4. One new law said that anybody helping an escaping slave would have to pay

_____ as a fine.

5. The U.S. government said that nobody could bring more slaves to America from

_____ .

6. After the law changed, slaves who wanted freedom had to run away to

_____ .

DIRECTIONS: Answer the question in complete sentences.

7. How did slaves help plantation owners make even more money? _____

_____

_____

TO CANADA!

DIRECTIONS: To learn more about slaves escaping to Canada and freedom in the 19th century, sing this song to the tune of "O, Susannah!"

I'M ON MY WAY TO CANADA

I'm on my way to Canada,
That cold and dreary land;
The sad effects of slavery,
I can no longer stand.

CHORUS:
Farewell, old master, don't think hard of me;
I'm on my way to Canada, where all the slaves are free.

The hounds are baying on my track;
Old master comes behind,
Resolved that he will bring me back,
Before I cross the line!

CHORUS:
Farewell, old master, don't think hard of me;
I'm on my way to Canada, where all the slaves are free.

I heard that Queen Victoria
Stands with arms held wide,
To give us all a peaceful home
Beyond the rolling tide.

CHORUS:
Farewell, old master, don't think hard of me;
I'm on my way to Canada, where all the slaves are free.

Name: _____ Date: _____

DIRECTIONS: In the Dred Scott case of 1857, African Americans were told that they were not citizens. Read each story and circle the answers to the questions.

1. John Jefferson is an African American. He lives in Ohio in 1855. He owns a store. A man named Wilbur Brooks owes John money. John tries everything he can to get Wilbur to pay. What is the best way John can get Wilbur to pay?

   a. ask Wilbur again
   b. try to steal the money back from Wilbur
   c. take Wilbur to court and ask a judge to tell Wilbur to pay him

   Now, it is 1859. Can John take Wilbur to court?   YES   NO

2. Maria Sanders is an African American. She lives in Boston in 1855. She was born free. She has lived in Boston her entire life. Slave hunters come to the Sanders house. They want to come inside and search it. They say that they think an escaped slave is living there. What is the best way Maria can keep the slave hunters out of her house?

   a. tell them they cannot come in
   b. send them to a judge who would decide if they could search
   c. run away

   Now, it is 1859. Can Maria Sanders send the slave hunters to a judge?   YES   NO

3. It is 1860. An African American named Charles Wilder gives a speech in New York saying that slavery is wrong. He is arrested and told that he can never speak against slavery again.

   Does Charles have the right to free speech?   YES   NO

4. In what other ways did the Dred Scott case change life for African Americans?

   _____

   _____

   _____

   _____

   _____

"That on the 1st day of January ... ny State or designated part of a State the people whereof shall then be ... States shall ... then, thenceforward, and forever free; and the executive go ... ment ... indi ... ... naval authority thereof, will recognize a ... ... repress such persons, or any of them, in any efforts they may ...

"That the executive will on the 1st day of January ... y proclamation, designate the States and parts of States, if any, in which the people thereof, respectively, shall then be in rebellion against the United States; and the fact that any State or the people thereof shall on ... be in good faith represented in the Congress of the United States by members chosen thereto at electio ... a majority of the qualified voters of such States shall have participated shall, in the absence of strong ... ... ailing testimony, be deemed conclusive evidence that such State and the people thereof are not then in rebellion against the United States."

Now, therefore, I, Abraham Lincoln, President of the United States, by virtue of the power in me vested as Commander-In-Chief of the Army and Navy of the United States in time of actual armed rebellion against the authority and government of the ... war measure for suppressing said ...

When the Civil War started, thousands of African Americans in the North wanted to join the Union army. At first, they were refused. President Lincoln opposed the idea of black men in the military. He wanted a gradual emancipation of slaves and did not feel that slavery was a central issue in the conflict. So, African Americans found other ways to contribute.

Some fleeing slaves, called "contraband" by the Union army, attached themselves to units and became part of the war effort. They performed duties that included acting as scouts and spies. Harriet Tubman also worked for the Union army as an organizer of a network of scouts and spies.

Other African Americans, still enslaved in the South, performed courageous acts of sabotage. One of these slaves, Robert Smalls, stole a Confederate steamship, along with ammunition, and delivered it into the hands of the Union navy. At the battle of Antietam, the Union army mysteriously obtained General Lee's battle plans. Many scholars believe that African Americans aided in this important event.

On July 17, 1862, Congress passed the Militia Act. This allowed the President to enlist "persons of African descent" into military service. In September of the same year, the Emancipation Proclamation (effective January 1, 1863) opened the way

for a flood of Union army volunteers from the African American community. The Confederate army also began recruiting black soldiers around this time. The position of free black soldiers in the North was extremely dangerous. Not only did they risk dying in battle, they also risked being taken into slavery. The South announced that any black soldier fighting for the North would be treated like a fugitive slave and "returned" to slavery if caught. Any Union officer in command of black soldiers would be shot. The new soldiers also had to fight for equal treatment. At first, African American soldiers were only paid about half of the amount that white soldiers were given. Some units, including the famous 54th Massachusetts, refused pay in protest until they were paid the same as white men. It was not until 1864 that Congress finally approved equal pay and back pay, but only for those African Americans who had been free at the time of enlistment.

Estimates vary as to the number of African Americans who enlisted in the army, but between 175,000 and 200,000 men served. This count does not include others, still enslaved in the South, who risked their lives to steal Confederate military secrets, destroy ammunition, and damage military buildings. Every African American in the United States had a huge stake in the outcome of the war. Their contributions made an important difference.

In addition to the racial challenges, African Americans in the Union Army also faced the same day-to-day hardships as white soldiers. This research exploration will help students examine the daily lives of Civil War soldiers when they were not doing battle.

FOLLOW THESE STEPS:

1. Have students look for photographs of and information about African American soldiers online or in a school media center. Talk about possible feelings the soldiers had. Were they proud to be soldiers? Were they fighting to end slavery? Had they ever been away from home before?

2. Have students find information about the daily lives of soldiers. Talk about what soldiers wore, where they lived, and what they ate. A soldier's life was much like year-round camping with boring food and a great amount of marching. How would students feel about leaving their homes to live like this?

3. Tell students that, at first, black soldiers were paid only half of the amount white soldiers received. How might they have felt about that? Tell students about the regiments that refused to accept pay in protest. Ask them if they think this tactic worked.

4. Distribute copies of the reproducible on page 51. Tell students to answer the questions based on class research and discussion. Ask each student to imagine himself in the role of an African American soldier. What are the good things about being a soldier? What are the bad or hard things?

5. Divide students into small groups. Have each group create and perform a skit. Each skit should portray a group of African American soldiers during the Civil War talking about their lives and their work as soldiers.

ROBERT SMALLS, HERO

Acts of sabotage by enslaved African Americans played a part in the Civil War, helping the Union troops from behind enemy lines. Perhaps no act of this kind was more dramatic than the capture of a steamer, the *Planter,* by a man named Robert Smalls. Smalls was a slave whose master sent him to work on the docks of Charleston Harbor. He was allowed to rent a house there, and he lived with his wife and children. When the war started, Smalls and his wife were saving money to buy their freedom. But, the war changed those plans. Smalls was an accomplished steamship pilot. He hatched a plan that would help the Union and win freedom for himself and his family at the same time. This activity will help students learn more about this Civil War hero.

FOLLOW THESE STEPS:

1. Distribute copies of the reproducible on page 52. (This article is based on accounts from Northern newspapers of the period but has been rewritten for grade-level appropriateness.) Have students read the article individually or as a class.

2. Have students find pictures of Robert Smalls and the *Planter* in library books or online. Next, have students find pictures of Charleston and Civil War period maps of its harbor. It is important for students to visualize Charleston's lengthy, sheltered harbor and how long it would take to steam across it from the docks.

3. Distribute copies of the reproducible on page 53. This worksheet will help students make the connection between the planning that went into Robert Smalls's daring escape and the execution of the event itself.

4. Discuss the planning process as a group. What advantages did Robert Smalls have that made it easier for him to plan his escape? (He had his own house where meetings could be held; he worked as a pilot and knew the area; he knew all of the signals to pass the forts; etc.)

5. Ask students to do more research on Robert Smalls. What happened to him after the *Planter* was surrendered? (He was given prize money for the ship's value and given the rank of captain.) What happened to him after the Civil War? (He became a U.S. Congressman). Have students create a bulletin board to honor this important Civil War hero.

A COUNTRY DIVIDED

STUDENT READING PASSAGE

DIRECTIONS: Read the story. Then, answer the questions.

The Civil War did not start because of slavery. It started because of **states' rights**. The states in the South felt that they had the right to leave, or secede from, the United States. The North felt that individual states did not have the power to make that choice.

For African Americans, slavery was the most important issue of the war. Many tried to join the Union army as soon as the war started. But, they could not. At the time, the law said that African Americans could not be soldiers. So, at the start of the war, they found other ways to help. Some escaped slaves stayed with Union soldiers to help them. Some African Americans were spies. Harriet Tubman went to the South to start a group of spies and scouts for the North.

The law changed in 1862, and thousands of African Americans signed up to be soldiers. About 200,000 African Americans

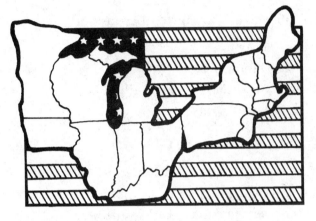

fought during the Civil War. They faced extreme danger in the army. The Southern army said that if they caught a black soldier, he would be treated like a runaway slave. He would be "sent back" to slavery—even if he was free!

African Americans wanted to help the North win the war. They felt it was their best chance to end slavery in the United States. They were right. In 1862, President Lincoln signed the **Emancipation Proclamation**. This said that any slave in a state that was fighting against the Union was now free. At the end of the war, slavery ended, too.

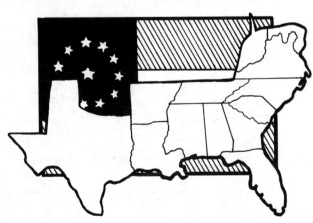

UNIT 6: THE CIVIL WAR
A COUNTRY DIVIDED
STUDENT READING QUESTIONS

DIRECTIONS: Circle the correct answers.

1. The Civil War started because of—

   a. slavery.
   b. plantations.
   c. the Underground Railroad.
   d. states' rights.

2. At the start of the Civil War, African Americans—

   a. went to their old homes in the South.
   b. could not join the Union army.
   c. were not interested in the war.
   d. none of the above

3. The law that freed slaves in the states that were fighting against the Union was—

   a. signed in 1862.
   b. signed by President Lincoln.
   c. called the Emancipation Proclamation.
   d. all of the above

DIRECTIONS: Fill in each blank with the correct answer.

4. About _____ African Americans fought in the Union army during the Civil War.

5. _____ started a group of spies in the South.

6. The states in the _____ said that they could leave the Union.

DIRECTIONS: Answer the question in complete sentences.

7. According to the Southern army, what might happen to an African American soldier in the Union Army during the Civil War?

   _____

   _____

   _____

Name: _____   Date: _____

DIRECTIONS: Pretend you are an African American soldier in the Union army during the Civil War. Use information that you found during your research to answer the questions.

1. What is the best thing about being a Union soldier?

   _____

   _____

   _____

   _____

   _____

2. What is the worst thing about being a Union soldier?

   _____

   _____

3. List four words that describe your tent home.

   _____   _____

   _____   _____

4. My favorite food that we eat in the army is _____

   _____ .

5. One food we eat in the army that I do not like is _____

   _____ .

6. Circle four words or phrases that best describe how you feel as a soldier.

   too cold   loyal   bored   hungry   sore feet

   tired   too hot   brave   scared   proud

Name: _____ Date: _____

UNIT 6: THE CIVIL WAR

ROBERT SMALLS, HERO

STUDENT ACTIVITY

DIRECTIONS: Read the newspaper article. Then, answer the questions.

DARING ESCAPE!

FORMER SLAVE, NOW FREE, STEALS BOAT FOR THE UNION

CHARLESTON, S.C., MAY 13, 1862—A Southern ship has been stolen! It was given to our navy by a slave named Robert Smalls. The ship is called the *Planter*. It was loaded with guns and ammunition that our navy can use. Mr. Smalls has brought us important news about the way the Charleston harbor is guarded. He also brought his family, his crew, and their families to freedom.

Mr. Smalls stole the ship in front of the guards at four Southern forts! How did he do it? Mr. Smalls worked as a ship's pilot on the *Planter*. He knows every inch of the harbor. Every night, the white men on the crew went home early. They would make the slaves finish cleaning the ship. This gave Mr. Smalls the idea of stealing the ship.

Mr. Smalls did not live with his master. He had his own house. He and the other slaves on the crew met at his house to plan their escape. Mr. Smalls knew how to give special signals to the guards at the forts. But, the crew knew that if the guards came onto the ship, they would be caught. They made a plan: if the guards stopped them, they would blow up the ship. Mr. Smalls told them it would be better to die as free people than be taken back to slavery.

On the night of May 12th, the white crew members went home. Mr. Smalls's wife and children and the wives and children of the other black crew members took a small boat from another dock. They rowed to a meeting place on the water. Mr. Smalls put on the captain's coat and hat. He walked and moved like the captain. A guard at one fort saw the *Planter* move slowly out into the harbor. It stopped for a minute. Then, it went on.

An hour later, the ship was close to Fort Sumter. It was the last fort. Soon, it would be daylight. When the sun came up, the guards in the fort would know that slaves, not white men, were sailing the ship. Beyond the fort were ships from the Northern navy. Mr. Smalls safely passed Fort Sumter by giving the secret signal. Then, he steered toward one of the Northern ships. How did the ship know the *Planter* was not going to attack it? Mrs. Smalls had a white bedsheet. Mr. Smalls took down the Southern flag. He put up the white sheet instead. That was a sign that the *Planter* was not going to fire.

When the captain of the navy boat *Onward* came on board, Mr. Smalls told him that he was giving the *Planter* to the North. He was also giving them guns, cannons, and ammunition that were on the ship. "I thought they might be of some service to Uncle Abe," said Mr. Smalls.

Mr. Smalls also had important news to tell about the guards and forts in the harbor. This might help our navy conquer these forts in the future. Meanwhile, we have a new hero for the North!

UNIT 6: THE CIVIL WAR
ROBERT SMALLS, HERO
STUDENT ACTIVITY QUESTIONS

DIRECTIONS: Answer the questions.

1. What two things did Robert Smalls want to do?

    _____

    _____

2. How did Robert Smalls plan to escape?

    _____

    _____

3. Why do you think the boat stopped for a minute after it left the dock?

    _____

    _____

4. Why did Robert Smalls know how to give the secret signals to the forts? _____

    _____

5. Robert Smalls tricked the guards by wearing _____

    _____ .

6. How did Robert Smalls let the Northern ships know he was not going to attack? _____

    _____

7. Besides the *Planter*, what else did Robert Smalls bring to the Northern navy? _____

    _____

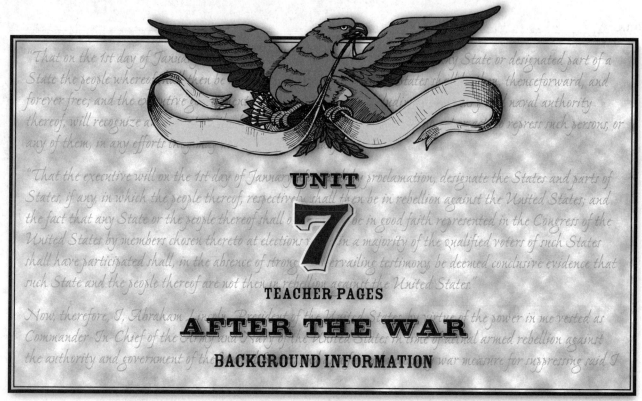

When the Civil War ended, many things changed for African Americans and for the country as a whole. When Congress passed the 13th Amendment, slavery in the United States was abolished. Congress also launched Reconstruction, a process by which Southern states would be taken back into the Union. One intent of Reconstruction was to help white people and black people live together in a newly free society. Another goal was to provide education to freed slaves who had been prevented from learning to read and write. Some former slaves chose to continue working for their former masters, but for wages. Others left the plantations to try to find family members who had been sold. The work of Reconstruction was too vast. In some ways, it was doomed to fail from the start. But, during the period of Reconstruction, many African Americans were free to vote, run for government offices, and start businesses.

The Southern states viewed the entire process of Reconstruction as punitive. Many white Southerners were appalled when African Americans were voted into various offices and started to participate in government. "Black codes," laws restricting civil rights, were immediately passed in many Southern states, only to be overturned by federal law. The 14th Amendment, passed in 1868, made it clear that African Americans were citizens. In 1870, the 15th Amendment gave African American men the right to vote.

In 1875, Congress passed a Civil Rights Act that said that African Americans, as well as white people, had the right to stay at inns, dine in restaurants, use public transportation, and go to theaters. However, in 1883, the Supreme Court ruled that the law was unconstitutional. African Americans, the Court said, only had the right of protection from discrimination from the state itself. Private business owners were free to keep black people from entering or using their premises. This opened the door for a wave of "jim crow" laws that established separate facilities, challenged voting rights, and even restricted other civil rights for black people.

As early as 1876, black voters were being turned away at polls in the South by intimidation and violence. Poll taxes and literacy tests also kept African Americans from voting. By the turn of the 20th century, many places in the South were hostile and dangerous for African Americans. However, Reconstruction did see the birth of a set of laws to protect African Americans. Later, during the civil rights movement, African Americans were able to build on this invaluable foundation.

A HUGE JOB

Reconstruction (1865–1877) is often termed a "failure" by historians. In fact, it was a highly complex and difficult period in U.S. history. The work of Reconstruction was so vast that failure, in one sense, was almost inevitable. But, a number of important things were accomplished during Reconstruction:

☞ Each state that rebelled against the Union was reaccepted through a legal process created by the federal government.

☞ Southern transportation and communications were reestablished (railroads, roads, and telegraph lines had been destroyed during the Civil War).

☞ Southern agriculture was reestablished.

☞ New schools were opened to educate freed slaves.

☞ African Americans held government posts, including seats in Congress.

☞ African American men were given the right to vote.

Help students understand the huge scope of Reconstruction with this exercise.

FOLLOW THESE STEPS:

1. Talk to students about war. What is a country like after a war? What kind of damage might there be? What problems might people have?

2. Next, talk specifically about the South after the Civil War. Use a map to show students where most of the fighting took place. Tell students that troops often took farm animals and destroyed fields. The Union cut north-south telegraph lines at the start of the war. Roads, bridges, and train tracks were also destroyed.

3. Talk about the freed slaves in the South. What would they need to start their new lives? How would they find their families? Where would they find jobs?

4. Be sure to talk to students about one of the chief goals of Reconstruction: the reacceptance of the Southern states into the Union. The states had to go through a process by which they accepted the new amendments to the Constitution and allowed Union soldiers to keep peace through military law.

5. Distribute copies of the reproducible on page 59. Tell students to imagine that they were elected to Congress just after the war ended. Have students rank the tasks of Reconstruction using 1 to show what they feel is the most important task, 2 to show the next in importance, etc. Students should find it very difficult, if not impossible, to assign ranks to these issues. After students have completed their worksheets, talk about how difficult it is to prioritize this list and why. Discuss why students assigned the ranks they did.

Vote

The period of Reconstruction and its aftermath was tumultuous, with many laws being passed by both the federal and state legislatures. Some of these laws aided African Americans and continue to do so. Others were very harmful to African Americans.

This activity is designed to help students understand the changing laws during this period in American history.

FOLLOW THESE STEPS:

1. Read the following text to students:

    Some laws passed during Reconstruction helped African Americans. The 13th Amendment gave them freedom. The 14th Amendment protected their rights as citizens. The 15th Amendment said that African American men could vote. The Civil Rights Act of 1875 said that African Americans could go to restaurants, theaters, stores, and other places just like white people.

    Other laws made life harder for African Americans. States in the South passed black codes, which were laws that took away rights. Each state had different laws. One law in Mississippi said that African Americans could not own land outside of cities. This meant they could not buy farms of their own. Another law said that any African American man who did not have a job had to go to jail. Black codes were overturned by the federal government.

After Reconstruction, more laws came into effect. The Civil Rights Act of 1875 was overturned by the Supreme Court. The Court said that places that were owned by private citizens, like stores or restaurants, were not required to serve African Americans. The South passed laws that made African Americans use separate schools, restrooms, and water fountains. Other new laws made it hard for African Americans to vote. They were forced to take difficult tests in some states. Other states said that African Americans had to pay to vote.

2. Distribute copies of the reproducible on page 60. This worksheet will give students an understanding of the literacy tests implemented in some Southern states. The questions on Test A are actually taken from period examples. Note the deliberately confusing wording of question 3 and the level of difficulty of the questions. The questions on Test B show alternative questions that would have made it easier to test literacy. Ask students what they think about each test. Which test is more fair?

3. After the class has worked with the voting tests and talked about other laws restricting African Americans, distribute copies of the reproducible on page 61. Students can use this worksheet to write a letter to the editor of a newspaper of the time. Have students choose one of the laws that have been discussed and write why they think it is a good or bad law. Have students share their letters with the class.

DIRECTIONS: Read the story. Then, answer the questions.

When the Civil War ended, there was a lot of work to do. The South needed to be rebuilt. Many farms and roads were ruined during the war. But, something else needed to be rebuilt, too—life in the South.

The slaves were free. What did this mean? It meant that African Americans could work for money. They could go to school and learn. They could live with their own families.

It also meant that white people had to learn to live with these big changes. Many people could. But, some did not want to. They were angry that there were no more slaves. They did not want African Americans to learn to read, to vote, or to work in government.

Laws were passed to help African Americans. Some of the laws were changes to the Constitution, called **amendments**. The 13th Amendment freed the slaves everywhere in the country. The 14th Amendment said that black people were citizens and had rights. The 15th Amendment said that African American men could vote.

Congress called this period in history **Reconstruction**. During this time, the South was rebuilt. Schools were started for former slaves. African Americans found new jobs. Some were even elected to Congress.

After Reconstruction ended in 1877, things started changing again. Some states in the South passed new laws. Some of these laws said that African Americans could not go to the same schools as white people. They could not sit at the fronts of buses or stay in hotels. There were also new laws to try to keep African Americans from voting. They had to pass hard tests or pay money to vote. Life for African Americans became hard again. They were free by law, but they did not always feel free.

Name: ______________________________ Date: ______________

UNIT 7: AFTER THE WAR

THE RIP THAT WOULD NOT MEND

STUDENT READING QUESTIONS

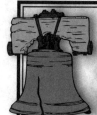

DIRECTIONS: Circle the correct answers.

1. The 13th Amendment—

   a. said African Americans could own homes.
   b. set all of the slaves in the United States free.
   c. established separate places for black people and white people.
   d. none of the above

2. **Reconstruction** ended in—

   a. 1865.
   b. 1977.
   c. 1857.
   d. 1877.

3. States kept African Americans from voting by—

   a. making them pay money to vote.
   b. making them pass hard tests.
   c. giving them voting passes.
   d. a. and b.

DIRECTIONS: Fill in each blank with the correct answer.

4. The ____________________ Amendment said that African American men could vote.

5. Life in the South needed to be ______________________________ after the war.

6. Some people in the South were angry because ______________________________

   ____.

DIRECTIONS: Answer the question in complete sentences.

7. What do you think was the hardest thing for African Americans after the Civil War ended?

   ____

   ____

   ____

Name: _____ Date: _____

UNIT 7: AFTER THE WAR

A HUGE JOB

STUDENT ACTIVITY

DIRECTIONS: Imagine you have been elected to Congress. It is 1866, and it is time to rebuild the country after the Civil War. You need to try to do all of the things on this chart. Rank them from 1 to 9 with number 1 being the most important, number 2 being the next in importance, and so on.

TASK	RANK (1-9)
help former slaves find their families	
teach former slaves to read and write	
rebuild all of the homes, stores, and other buildings that were burned or bombed in the South	
help former slaves find new jobs	
make sure that all African American men can vote	
fix ruined farms so that people can grow food again	
reestablish the money system in the South so that people can buy things again	
fix the roads and railroads so that the goods needed for rebuilding can be sent from the North to the South	
take the Southern states back into the Union so that they are part of the United States again	

Name: _____ Date: _____

DIRECTIONS: Answer the questions for each test. If you get one question wrong, you cannot vote.

TEST A	TEST B
1. Who is the Attorney General of the United States? _____	1. Who was the first president of the United States? _____
2. Name one area of authority over state militia reserved exclusively to the states. _____	2. Name ONE right you have as a citizen of the United States. _____
3. In the space below, write the word NOISE backward and place a dot over what would be its second letter should it have been written forward. _____	3. Write the name of our state on the line. _____
4. Give your age in days. _____	4. How old are you? _____ years old

5. Which test would you rather take? (Circle one.)   **TEST A**   **TEST B**

   Why? _____

   _____

   _____

6. Which test do you think was given to African Americans? Explain your answer.

   _____

   _____

   _____

UNIT 7: AFTER THE WAR
LETTER TO THE EDITOR
STUDENT ACTIVITY

DIRECTIONS: You have decided to write a letter to a local newspaper. You want to write about one of the new laws that have passed since the Civil War. You can write about a law that helps African Americans or hurts them. Tell the editor about the law. Then, explain why you do or do not like the law.

Dear Editor,

I am writing to you about _____.
(Write the name of the law or describe it.)

_____

_____

The result of this new law will be _____
(Tell what the law does.)

_____

_____

I think that this law is a   **GOOD IDEA**   **BAD IDEA**
(Circle one.)

because _____
(Tell how you feel about the new law.)

_____

_____

Very truly yours,

_____
(Sign your name.)

Civil rights laws began to unravel after Reconstruction ended. States started passing jim crow laws allowing segregation of most facilities. The Supreme Court, in its decision for *Plessy v. Ferguson* in 1896, decreed that segregation was legal as long as "separate but equal" facilities existed. However, few facilities for African Americans were equal, or even adequate, compared to those available to white people.

African Americans attended separate schools, sat at the backs of buses, and experienced difficulties finding places to stay while on vacation. In the South, they were forced to use separate doorways, drink from different water fountains, and step into gutters when passing white people on sidewalks. Every aspect of daily life was orchestrated to show African Americans that they were second-class citizens.

Linda Brown of Topeka, Kansas, had to walk past a white school and then hike a mile through a dangerous neighborhood, crossing high-traffic streets and a railroad switching station to go to school. That walk alone demonstrated the fallacy of "separate but equal." When her case was heard in the Supreme Court in 1954, the justices ruled that segregation of schools was unconstitutional.

This ruling opened the doors for a massive civil rights movement, the purpose of which was to test other constraints placed on the rights of black people. In 1955, Rosa Parks was arrested after refusing to give her seat on a bus to a white man. The next year, The Reverend Dr. Martin Luther King, Jr., began organizing the civil rights movement. There was an attempt to block school segregation in Little Rock, Arkansas, which was met by federal troops. During a 1963 demonstration, hoses and police dogs were turned on protestors. That was the same year Martin Luther King delivered his famous speech on the steps of the Lincoln Memorial. Many civil rights leaders and workers were killed in the years that followed, including Dr. King, who was assassinated in 1968.

In the face of intimidation, the movement held firm and gained legal ground. Poll taxes and literacy tests were outlawed. Federal laws stated that public "accommodations," such as hotels and restaurants, had to be open to all citizens, regardless of race. Even so, civil rights work is not finished and still continues. As recently as 2003, the Supreme Court upheld the right of universities to apply affirmative action while selecting students.

IS "SEPARATE BUT EQUAL" REALLY EQUAL?

The concept of "separate but equal" is central to understanding why segregation laws put African Americans at such a disadvantage. Separate facilities for black people were seldom "equal" to the facilities for white people. This was particularly true of schools. African American students walked while white children rode buses. Teachers were often paid as much as 40 percent less at black schools than at white schools. Books, supplies, and even chairs were scarce in African American schools. In some school districts, African American parents actually had to build school buildings for their children because the district refused to supply them.

The Supreme Court ruled in 1954 that separate facilities are inherently unequal. But, in reality, they were also literally unequal. This is something you can help students understand by playing this simple game.

FOLLOW THESE STEPS:

1. Randomly distribute checkers to students, one per student. Then, announce that all of the students with black checkers will move to the desks at the front of the classroom (or in favorite places in the classroom if you do not have a traditional desk setup). Red-checker students must sit in the back.

2. Start teaching a regular lesson. Interrupt the lesson to announce that red-checker students are losing half of their seats. They will now have to take turns sitting in chairs.

3. Resume teaching. At another pause, tell the red-checker students that they will have to give up half of their books, paper, or other items they need for class. Give the extra books and supplies to the black-checker students.

4. Continue to take things from the red-checker students for the remainder of the lesson. They could lose additional seats, have to stand at the back of the classroom, or have to share one book among three students. During all of this, the black-checker students should experience no adverse changes in their learning experience.

5. Return the classroom to normal. Then, distribute copies of the reproducible on page 67. Have students answer the questions.

6. Discuss the experience of the game with the class. How did the red-checker students feel? How did the black-checker students feel? Was this a good experience for anyone?

7. Introduce the history of the "separate but equal" law. Explain why this premise did not actually work in practice.

The civil rights movement was fueled by passionate beliefs and ideas about what was just and fair and about what it meant to be an American. In this activity, students will hear the words of civil rights leaders and then design a poster that expresses an idea from the movement in their own words.

FOLLOW THESE STEPS:

1. Read quotations or even segments of speeches from the civil rights movement to students. There are many famous speeches posted on the Internet. Discuss the meanings of the statements. Use the following quotations as discussion starters, as well:

"We shall overcome."

—**Civil rights movement song**

"You can kill a man, but you can't kill an idea."

—**Medgar Evers**

"You can't separate peace from freedom because no one can be at peace unless he has his freedom."

—**Malcolm X**

"Hating people because of their color is wrong. And, it doesn't matter which color does the hating. It's just plain wrong."

—**Muhammad Ali**

"America is not like a blanket— one piece of unbroken cloth, the same color, the same texture, the same size. America is more like a quilt—many patches, many pieces, many colors, many sizes, all woven and held together by a common thread."

—**Rev. Jesse Jackson**

"Knowing what must be done does away with fear."

—**Rosa Parks**

2. Distribute copies of the reproducibles on pages 68–69. Explain that students will design their own civil rights posters. Each student should use the slogan that she writes on page 68 as the central element of her poster. Students can use the clip art to add to their posters, or they can create their own art.

3. Posters can be 8 ½" x 11" (21.5 cm x 28 cm) or larger if poster board is available. Supply students with art materials and construction paper as they work on their posters.

4. Have each student give a brief presentation to show his poster to the class.

THE LONG WALK TO FREEDOM

DIRECTIONS: Read the story. Then, answer the questions.

By the 1900s, African Americans lived separate lives in the United States. They went to different schools from white people. They had to sit at the backs of buses and trains or stand up if white people wanted their seats. Sometimes, they even had to use different doors to go into buildings.

The law at the time said that this was all right, as long as the separate places were "equal." The problem was, they usually were not equal. Schools and other places for black people were not as good.

All of this started to change because of a third grader named Linda Brown. Linda had to walk right past an all-white school that was near her home. Then, she had to walk a mile to her own school. She had to walk through a dangerous neighborhood. She had to cross a railroad yard and busy streets. Her case went to the Supreme Court. Could Linda go to the school near her house?

When the Court said yes, it also said that it was not fair for white children and black children to have separate schools. This ruling started the **civil rights movement**. African American leaders like Dr. Martin Luther King, Jr., started working for better laws. Rosa Parks would not let a white man take her seat on a bus. Other African Americans went to all-white restaurants to eat. They went to **protest marches** where they walked in big groups. They held signs and posters to show what they wanted. It was dangerous. Some people were hurt. Others, like Dr. King, were killed.

But, these brave people were able to get the laws changed. New laws said that African Americans could eat, work, and relax in the same places as white people. They no longer had to take tests and pay money to vote. Now, they were full citizens with the same rights as white people.

Name: _____ Date: _____

DIRECTIONS: Circle the correct answers.

1. Linda Brown—

   a. could not go to the school near her home.
   b. had to walk across a railroad yard to school.
   c. had to walk a mile to school.
   d. all of the above

2. If you were African American in 1950, you might have to—

   a. give up your seat on a train if a white person wanted it.
   b. walk into a building by using a different door from white people.
   c. go to school with white people.
   d. a. and b.

3. The **civil rights movement**—

   a. started because laws were unfair to white people.
   b. said that African Americans should have the same rights as white people.
   c. was led by a person named Linda Brown.
   d. none of the above

DIRECTIONS: Fill in each blank with the correct answer.

4. One leader of the civil rights movement was named _____ .

5. A **protest march** happens when people march and carry _____ to show what they want.

6. _____ became famous when she would not give up her seat on a bus.

DIRECTIONS: Write your answer in complete sentences.

7. Name and describe one law that changed because of the civil rights movement. _____

   _____

   _____

   _____

UNIT 8: CIVIL RIGHTS

IS "SEPARATE BUT EQUAL" REALLY EQUAL?

STUDENT ACTIVITY QUESTIONS

DIRECTIONS: Answer the questions.

1. What color checker did you have? _____

2. Where did you sit in the classroom? _____

3. Was the place you sat better or worse than your normal seat? _____

   Why? _____

   _____

   _____

4. How did you feel when the red-checker students started to lose things they needed for class?

   _____

   _____

   _____

5. What did the red-checker students lose that made their situation the hardest?

   _____

6. After a while, how did you feel about the red-checker students—either about them or about being one of them? Explain your answer.

   _____

   _____

   _____

   _____

7. Did you want to change places with a student from the other group? **YES**   **NO**

   Why or why not? _____

   _____

   _____

PUTTING IT INTO PRACTICE

STUDENT ACTIVITY

DIRECTIONS: Answer the questions.

1. What do you think was the most important theme of the civil rights movement? _____
   _____

2. Why do you think this theme was and is important for all people? _____
   _____
   _____
   _____

3. How would you talk about this theme in just one or two words? _____

4. What colors will you use on the poster? _____

5. What do you want people to understand when they see the poster? _____
   _____
   _____

6. Use the space below to plan your poster. Make sure the words that describe the theme are the largest thing on the poster. Then, make your poster on a piece of paper or poster board.

UNIT 8: CIVIL RIGHTS

PUTTING IT INTO PRACTICE

STUDENT ACTIVITY

DIRECTIONS: Use the clip art to decorate your civil rights poster.

Preserving cultural traditions is especially important for many African Americans. While many Americans are able to trace their family histories, this information is much harder for African Americans to find. African Americans were not listed by name in a census until 1870. Slaves were counted as property, so they were rarely named as individuals, and they were never listed in family groups. It is ironic that most African Americans have deeper roots in America than many white people, most of whom descended from more recent immigrants. Yet, in many cases, the roots of African American families are difficult to uncover.

There are some sources that can help. One of the strong traditions in many African cultures is storytelling. In West Africa, a tribal *griot* is responsible not only for relating legends of importance and teaching tales, but also for telling the stories of the families within a tribe. This oral history encompasses generations of families: their births, marriages, dreams, battles, and deaths. Many Africans who were enslaved and brought to the United States continued the responsibility of telling stories about their family members. Sometimes, it was all they could give their children to maintain family continuity.

Some African Americans have actually been able to use their own families' oral histories to trace genealogical facts and cultural roots to Africa.

An extension of this storytelling tradition was the creation of family histories on quilts. Once they were in America, some African American women used quilting as a medium not only for art, but also to preserve family stories in a pictorial form. Since slaves were forbidden to read and write, these pictures provided a more permanent record of family history.

African Americans have also created unique holidays that relate to specific historical events and cultural traditions. Juneteenth, the celebration of the day when slaves in Texas learned that they had been freed by the Emancipation Proclamation, is a summer holiday in many places across the United States. Kwanzaa, a festival of family and community, was created by Dr. Maulana Karenga in 1966. Its intent is to bring African Americans together to appreciate both their roots and their communities. It is celebrated from December 26 to January 1. Events like these preserve the importance of specific traditions for African Americans today.

African Americans have connected with their heritage in a number of important ways, such as the creation of meaningful holidays. Martin Luther King Day and Kwanzaa are two examples of this; another is Juneteenth. In this activity, students will learn about Juneteenth and then plan a Juneteenth celebration.

FOLLOW THESE STEPS:

1. Read the following history of Juneteenth to students.

   June 19, 1865, was a hot day in Galveston, Texas. A ship, led by General Gordon Granger, brought Union soldiers to the city. During the long Civil War, the slaves in Texas had not seen many Union soldiers. They had not received much news about the war. But, General Gordon had amazing news. The war was over! The Union won! The most amazing news of all was that the slaves were free! Nobody had told the slaves in Texas about the Emancipation Proclamation, President Lincoln's order that freed slaves in rebel states two years earlier. Now, slaves across the country knew about their freedom. So, June 19, 1865, was the true beginning of freedom for all African Americans.

   The newly freed people celebrated on that day and every year on June 19. What were those early Juneteenth parties like? African Americans kept their traditions of telling stories and listening to their elders. There were always people who spoke at the parties and recalled what it was like to be held as
   slaves. Sometimes, important people would come to speak about the gift of freedom. Because slaves had been forced to wear dull, worn-out clothes, African Americans often wore bright colors and new clothes to celebrate Juneteenth. Special foods were served. Meat like lamb and pork was cooked over open fires, just like it had been long ago in Africa. Strawberry soda was a brand-new drink in the late 19th century and a real treat. It became the favorite drink at Juneteenth celebrations. People always danced like the slaves did when they first heard the news that they were free. People sang songs they had learned from their families. It was a day to remember the terrible time of slavery and to be full of joy that freedom had come.

2. Have students use the Internet or local library resources to investigate how many Juneteenth celebrations are held today. Today, over 200 cities celebrate Juneteenth. A few states have made June 19 a state holiday. There is a campaign to make the day a national holiday.

3. Ask students to think about what kind of party they would like to attend to celebrate Juneteenth. Is there a way to plan a party that would be fun today and also connect to the early celebrations? Divide students into small groups. Distribute copies of the reproducible on page 75. Have students work together to brainstorm ideas for their own Juneteenth parties.

4. Ask each small group to make a presentation about their Juneteenth celebration party.

FAMILY HISTORY IS ALIVE!

Family history is important to almost everyone, but it has special and specific meaning for many African American families. In this activity, you can demonstrate the importance of oral family stories and the African American tradition of making family history quilts.

FOLLOW THESE STEPS:

1. Talk to students about the tradition of oral family stories in many African tribes. Talk about the importance of this tradition for enslaved families who were forbidden to read and write as they faced the reality of sudden separation.

2. Next, talk to students about their own family stories. How much do they know about their own family histories? What stories are important to them? Ask them to think about what they know about their ancestors, their family histories, and more recent events in their families.

3. Distribute copies of the reproducible on page 76. This worksheet will help each student conduct an interview with a member of his family. From this interview, it is important that the student gets a sense of his family's stories—the events that have been shared across generations.

4. After students have completed their interviews, talk with them about the African American tradition of family history quilts. Tell them that they will use four stories about themselves and their families to create a quilt design. Distribute copies of the reproducible on page 77. Explain that the diamond border separating the quilt blocks is an African American tradition. Since the diamond represents the life cycle (birth, life, death, and rebirth), this design is especially appropriate for a family history quilt. Show them pictures of actual family history quilts to help them visualize this concept.

5. After students have drawn pictures of their four chosen stories, have them make the actual quilt "blocks" out of construction paper. Blocks can be decorated with markers, crayons, paint, or torn paper. Assemble a class quilt, using a paper border with a diamond design to separate the blocks.

DIRECTIONS: Read the story. Then, answer the questions.

How did slave families preserve their family histories? They did it the same way that we do today: by telling stories. This was an important part of slaves' lives. Stories about family helped children remember their parents and **ancestors**, the long-ago people in their families. This was especially important if children and parents were sold away from each other. Some slave families also sewed quilts. The quilts showed pictures of things that happened to members of their families. Because many slaves were not allowed to read or write, these quilts helped keep a record of family stories.

African Americans today have used family stories, and sometimes even things like quilts, to find out more about their family roots.

Storytelling is important to many Africans. In West Africa, each tribe has a story-teller, called a **griot**. Griots do not just tell tales and legends. They are also responsible for remembering the histories of their tribes. These stories tell about each family's children, marriages, and big events. When people were taken from Africa and sent to America as slaves, many of them kept this storytelling alive for their own children.

African Americans have also made new holidays that help them honor the past. Juneteenth is an important summer holiday. It started two years after the Emancipation Proclamation when slaves in Texas learned they had been freed. Today, many communities still hold Juneteenth parties on June 19.

Kwanzaa is a winter holiday. It was started in 1966 as a way to help African American families celebrate their families and communities. Each day of Kwanzaa is about a different strength or value. The holiday lasts from December 26 to January 1.

UNIT 9: BACK TO BEGINNINGS

ROOTS IN AFRICA

STUDENT READING QUESTIONS

DIRECTIONS: Circle the correct answers.

1. A **griot** is—

    a. a storyteller.
    b. a doctor.
    c. a cook.
    d. none of the above

2. Family stories were important to slave families because—

    a. one person in the family could be sold away from the rest.
    b. many slaves came from places where storytelling was important.
    c. slaves were usually not able to write down information about their families.
    d. all of the above

3. Juneteenth—

    a. is a summer holiday.
    b. started when slaves in Texas learned they were free.
    c. lasts for seven days.
    d. a. and b.

DIRECTIONS: Fill in each blank with the correct answer.

4. The winter holiday that was started in 1966 is called _____ .

5. **Ancestors** are_____ .

6. Some slaves made _____ that showed events from their family histories.

DIRECTIONS: Answer the questions.

7. What holiday is important in your family? What is one thing you do on that holiday?

    _____

    _____

    _____

    _____

UNIT 9: BACK TO BEGINNINGS
PLAN A JUNETEENTH PARTY!
STUDENT ACTIVITY QUESTIONS

DIRECTIONS: Think about what you know about the first Juneteenth parties. Talk about the questions with your group and write your answers. Think about how you can have both new things and things from the past at your party.

1. Where will you have your Juneteenth party? _____

    _____

2. What kind of music will you have at the party? _____

    _____

3. Circle four things that you might like to do at the party.

    sing songs   play volleyball   play baseball

    have a parade   have carnival rides   have a rodeo

    have fireworks   go fishing   have a big dance

4. What kind of food will you have at the party? Talk about your choices. List four things your group has chosen.

    _____   _____

    _____   _____

5. Telling stories and giving speeches are important at Juneteenth parties. If you could ask anyone to come to your party and tell a story or give a speech, who would you choose? Why?

    _____

    _____

    _____

    _____

    _____

Name: _____ Date: _____

DIRECTIONS: Choose someone in your family to interview. An older person in your family may know more about your family's history than a younger person. Ask the person these questions and record the answers.

1. What is your name? _____

2. What were/are your parents' names? _____

    _____

3. What were/are your parents' parents' names?

    Mother's parents: _____

    Father's parents: _____

4. Tell a story about something that happened to you when you were young. (Make notes
    here while the story is being told.) _____

    _____

    _____

5. Tell a story that one of your parents told you about his or her family. (Make notes here
    while story is being told.) _____

    _____

    _____

6. Where is your family from? _____

    Choose four words to describe the place where you grew up.

    _____   _____

    _____   _____

7. What is one place that is very important to our family? _____

    Why is it important? _____

    _____

UNIT 9: BACK TO BEGINNINGS

MY FAMILY HISTORY QUILT

STUDENT ACTIVITY

DIRECTIONS: Make your own family history quilt. Draw one picture in each square.

1. the most important day in your life
2. a place that is important to your family
3. something important that happened to your parents
4. an old family story

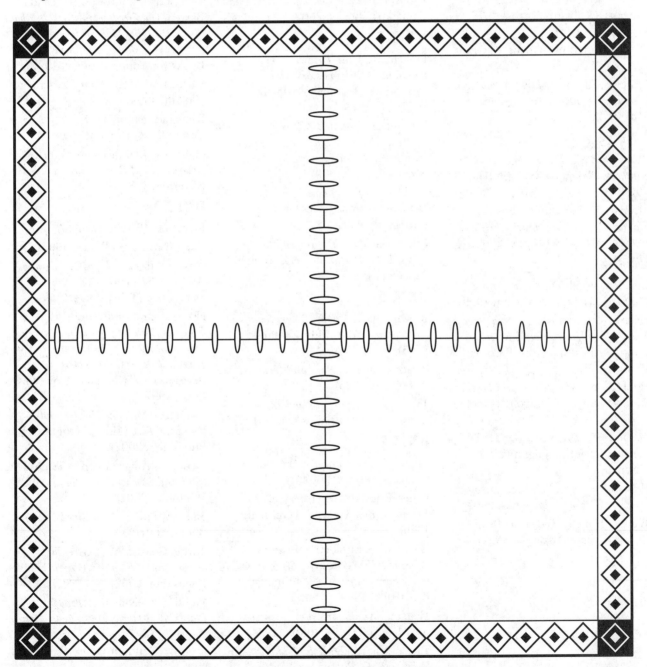

RESOURCES

UNIT 1

Alderman, Clifford L. *Colonists for Sale: The Story of Indentured Servants in America*. (Macmillan, 1975)

Galenson, David W. *White Servitude in Colonial America: An Economic Analysis*. (Cambridge University Press, 1981)

Lester, Julius. *To Be a Slave*. (Puffin, 2000)

Raskin, Joseph. *Tales of Indentured Servants*. (William Morrow, 1978)

Slavery and the Making of America, DVD, directed by William R. Grant (2005; PBS)

Watkins, Richard. *Slavery: Bondage Throughout History*. (Houghton Mifflin, 2001)

UNIT 2

Erickson, Paul. *Daily Life on a Southern Plantation 1853*. (Puffin, 2000)

McKissack, Patricia and Frederick. *Christmas in the Big House, Christmas in the Quarters*. (Scholastic, 2002)

UNIT 3

Bial, Raymond. *The Underground Railroad*. (Houghton Mifflin, 1999)

Harris, Kim and Reggie. *Steal Away: Music of the Underground Railroad*, compact disc (Appleseed Records, 1998).

Hopkinson, Deborah. *Sweet Clara and the Freedom Quilt*. (Dragonfly Books, 1995)

The Journey of August King, DVD, directed by John Duigan (2003; Miramax)

Nelson, Vaunda Micheaux. *Almost to Freedom*. (Carolrhoda Books, 2003)

Winter, Jeanette. *Follow the Drinking Gourd*. (Dragonfly Books, 1992)

UNIT 4

Buckmaster, Henrietta. *Let My People Go*. (University of South Carolina Press, 1992)

De Angeli, Marguerite. *Thee, Hannah!* (Herald Press, 2000)

Miller, William. *Frederick Douglass: The Last Day of Slavery*. (Sagebrush Bound, 1999)

Rockwell, Anne. *Only Passing Through: The Story of Sojourner Truth*. (Dragonfly Books, 2002)

UNIT 5

Finkelman, Paul. *Dred Scott v. Sandford: A Brief History with Documents*. (Bedford/St. Martin's, 1997)

Freedman, Florence B. *Two Tickets to Freedom: The True Story of Ellen and William Craft, Fugitive Slaves*. (Peter Bedrick Books, 1999)

Gunderson, Cory. *The Dred Scott Decision*. (Abdo & Daughters Publishing, 2004)

Potter, David M. *The Impending Crisis, 1848–1861*. (Harper Perennial Paperbacks, 1977)

UNIT 6

Brown, Susan Taylor. *Robert Smalls Sails to Freedom*. (Millbrook Press, 2005)

Polacco, Patricia. *Pink and Say*. (Scholastic, 1995)

Taylor, M. W. *Harriet Tubman: Antislavery Activist* (Sagebrush, 1999)

UNIT 7

English, Karen. *Francie*. (Farrar, Straus, & Giroux, 2002)

Foner, Eric. *A Short History of Reconstruction*. (Harper Perennial, 1990)

Hale, Grace Elizabeth. *Making Whiteness: The Culture of Segregation in the South, 1890–1940*. (Vintage Paperback, 1999)

Mettger, Zak. *Reconstruction: America After the Civil War*. (Dutton, 1994)

Taylor, Mildred D. *Roll of Thunder, Hear My Cry*. (Puffin Books, 1991)

UNIT 8

Bridges, Ruby. *Through My Eyes*. (Scholastic, 1999)

Coles, Robert. *The Story of Ruby Bridges*. (Scholastic, 2004)

Hampton, Henry; Fayer, Steve; and Flynn, Sarah. *Voices of Freedom: An Oral History of the Civil Rights Movement from the 1950s through the 1980s*. (Bantam, 1991)

King, Casey and Osborne, Linda Barrett. *Oh, Freedom!: Kids Talk About the Civil Rights Movement with the People Who Made It Happen*. (Knopf Books for Young Readers, 1997)

Parks, Rosa. *I Am Rosa Parks*. (Puffin, 1999)

Ringgold, Faith. *My Dream of Martin Luther King*. (Dragonfly, 1998)

Williams, Juan. *Eyes on the Prize: America's Civil Rights Years, 1954–1965*. (Penguin, 1988)

UNIT 9

Flournoy, Valerie. *The Patchwork Quilt*. (Gardeners Books, 1995)

Goss, Linda. *Talk That Talk: An Anthology of African-American Storytelling*. (Touchstone, 1989)

Horton, James Oliver and Lois E. (eds.) *A History of the African American People: The History, Traditions, and Culture of African Americans*. (Wayne State University Press, 1997)

LaTeef, Nelda. *The Hunter and the Ebony Tree*. (Moon Mountain Publishing, 2002)

Medearis, Angela Shelf. *Seven Spools of Thread: A Kwanzaa Story*. (Albert Whitman, 2004)

Tademy, Lalita. *Cane River*. (Warner Books, 2001)

Taylor, Charles A. *Juneteenth: A Celebration of Freedom*. (Open Hand Publishing, 2002)

Woodtor, Dee Parmer. *Finding a Place Called Home: A Guide to African-American Genealogy and Historical Identity*. (Random House Reference, 1999)

ANSWER KEY

PAGE 10 · SERVANTS AND SLAVES

1. d.
2. b.
3. Indentured servants were freed and given land and a house to start a new life when their indenture was complete.
4. F
5. T
6. F
7. F
8. Answers will vary.

PAGE 12 · FROM SERVANT TO SLAVE

Students' Venn diagrams should include the following information:

James: from Scotland

Victor: from Holland

John: from Africa

All three men: were indentured servants, were farm workers who worked in the fields, and ran away

James and Victor: had to serve four more years as a punishment for running away

John: had to serve his master for the rest of his life (became a slave) as a punishment for running away

PAGE 13 · FROM SERVANT TO SLAVE

1. d.
2. a.
3. John Punch was no longer a servant; he became a slave. He was a slave because his indenture would never end.
4. Answers will vary.
5. Answers will vary.
6. Answers will vary.

PAGE 18 · PLANTATION LIFE

1. d.
2. d.
3. Answers will vary.
4. F
5. F
6. F
7. T
8. Answers will vary.

PAGE 20 · A HOME IN THE SLAVE QUARTERS

1. Answers will vary. The family will need at least two more beds. Additional beds were usually made by covering straw with a cloth and putting this pallet on the floor.
2. Answers will vary. Items might include: plates or bowls, eating utensils, a frying pan, etc. They could hand carve utensils and dishes, or trade homemade quilts or other crafts for additional needs.
3. Answers will vary. Students might mention a table and chairs as a need. Answers will vary about how to make or trade for the furniture.
4. Answers will vary. Students should realize that the cabin will be very crowded and lack most amenities, so the answer will probably be no.

PAGE 26 · ESCAPE!

1. d.
2. c.
3. b.
4. T
5. F
6. T
7. T
8. Answers will vary but may include: building houses with secret hiding places, marking paths, and giving slaves fresh clothing and food.

PAGE 29 · PLAN YOUR ESCAPE

1. Answers will vary.
2. Answers will vary.
3. Answers will vary.
4. Answers will vary but may include: being caught because of the loud dogs outside of Pearson's Trading Post and Jones's farmhouse; being caught by the slave hunters at the trading post; being caught by the hunters in Middle Woods; being caught near the plantation; being caught by the owner of Cooper's Chicken Farm.
5. Answers will vary but may include: the plantation kitchen, the smokehouse, or Miss Smith's house. Miss Smith's house is probably the safest because it is not next to a plantation.
6. Answers will vary but may include: Miss Smith's house, the church, and possibly the empty cabin.

ANSWER KEY

PAGE 34 · SPEAKING OUT

1. c.
2. d.
3. d.
4. T
5. F
6. F
7. T
8. Answers will vary but may include: newspapers, books, and speeches.

PAGE 43 · TWO SIDES, NO MIDDLE

1. b.
2. d.
3. b.
4. $1,000
5. Africa
6. Canada
7. Answers will vary but should include the fact that slaves were not paid for their work.

PAGE 45 · DRED SCOTT: PERSON OR PROPERTY?

1. c., NO
2. b., NO
3. NO
4. Answers will vary, but discussion should reflect loss of other rights and connect to students' understanding of their own rights.

PAGE 50 · A COUNTRY DIVIDED

1. d.
2. b.
3. d.
4. 200,000
5. Harriet Tubman
6. South
7. Answers will vary but may include that he might be captured and sent into slavery.

PAGE 53 · ROBERT SMALLS, HERO

1. He wanted to help the Union and free his family and friends.
2. He planned to steal the steamship *Planter*.
3. The ship stopped to pick up the family members who rowed out to meet the *Planter*.
4. He knew the signals because he was a pilot in the harbor and had used them before.
5. the captain's hat and coat
6. He replaced the Southern flag with a white bedsheet to show that they would not fire.
7. Answers will vary but may include: guns, cannons, and ammunition as well as important news about the forts and harbor.

PAGE 58 · THE RIP THAT WOULD NOT MEND

1. b.
2. d.
3. d.
4. 15th
5. rebuilt
6. Answers will vary but may include: There were no more slaves; African Americans now had to be paid; African Americans were voted into government.
7. Answers will vary.

PAGE 66 · THE LONG WALK TO FREEDOM

1. d.
2. d.
3. b.
4. Answers will vary but may include: Dr. Martin Luther King, Jr., or Rosa Parks
5. signs and posters
6. Rosa Parks
7. Answers will vary but may include: paying to vote; taking hard tests to vote; being able to eat, work, and relax in the same places as white people.

PAGE 74 · ROOTS IN AFRICA

1. a.
2. d.
3. d.
4. Kwanzaa
5. family members from long ago
6. quilts
7. Answers will vary.